M000196434

ALL CHILDREN SMILE IN THE SAME LANGUAGE

ALL CHILDREN SMILE IN THE SAME LANGUAGE

A TEACHER'S JOURNEY

Daniel Bisaccio

gatekeeper press™

Columbus, Ohio

ALL CHILDREN SMILE IN THE SAME LANGUAGE:
A teacher's journey

Published by Gatekeeper Press
2167 Stringtown Rd, Suite 109
Columbus, OH 43123-2989
www.GatekeeperPress.com

The editorial work for this book is entirely the product of the author. Gatekeeper Press did not participate in and is not responsible for any aspect of this element.

Library of Congress Control Number: 2022937256

ISBN (hardcover): 9781662927935
eISBN: 9781662927959

This book is dedicated to the many teachers who are on the forefront of tomorrow. Teachers engage the future through the work they do each day with young minds and spirits who are our hope for a more just and humane global community.

Table of Contents

Preface

Dear Dan,

Once I knew you were leaving Souhegan High School for Brown University, I began writing down what I considered were your "lessons" about the art of teaching. I thought I would be thanking you for some of these "lessons" in a farewell card, but as I collected more than two or three, I thought "your lessons" or "words of wisdom" were really more like your "scientific laws of teaching."

The list of advice in Dan's Laws of Teaching came to me as I reflected on you as my mentor. Many of the laws that I recounted were literally words you had spoken during the time we spent together at Souhegan High School. I loved that some bordered on irreverent yet were so honest and pointed, such as likening teens to teaching hormones. As a horse lover for years, I laughed at your suggestion that a clean stall is the sign of a dead horse. Other ideas for laws came to me as I thought of your practice and what you instilled in us as colleagues. Other laws on that list continue to resonate with me to this day even after 22 years of teaching, such as trusting that a lesson idea is worth doing even if it isn't all figured out yet.

Whether I refer to your ideas on that document as lessons, insights, or "laws", they were most importantly gifts that you gave us to use every day we entered the classroom.

Thank you, Anne C-W.

Dan Bisaccio's Laws of Teaching

1. A clean stall means a dead horse.
2. Trying out an idea that is not perfected is better than not having tried it at all.
3. The best classroom is nature's classroom.
4. Time spent forming personal connections with students is far more important than time spent grading their work.
5. Integrity means being true to your vision and your students even if your boss disagrees.
6. Maintain the belief that every student and every colleague have the best intentions and believe that everyone else does the same.
7. Always wear a smile for kids, and if that doesn't work, recount a great anecdote … tell a story.
8. Nothing is more important than your family.
9. Take time to attend a professional conference and come back invigorated.
10. When all else fails, remember, "You are not really teaching kids, you are actually teaching adolescent hormones."

Introduction

As I am writing this, we are in year three of a global pandemic. The pandemic's impact on education is already emerging and I suspect will be fodder for numerous research papers in the coming years. One aspect of the impact is teacher "fallout" from the profession. Teachers are leaving the profession in record numbers. Retirement, early retirement, and even beginning to mid-career professionals have decided to leave teaching. I worry about this.

So, how do we attract vibrant, creative, and intelligent individuals to this most important profession? How do we retain the many outstanding teachers who may be considering leaving this profession? Smart people need to be engaged and create. Instead of writing "scripted curriculum" for a teacher to follow or devise new testing strategies to hold teachers accountable, our focus should be on strategies to engage novice teachers in using their academic content and pedagogical skills to create opportunities (curriculum) in which their students may surprise everyone. Teachers become artists in developing story lines for their evolving curriculum that fosters student passion for learning while mentoring their students. This approach not only engages students but will keep teachers intellectually engaged in their profession.

The core of the struggle between "why I want to teach" and the parameters that are both in place in schools as well as inflicted on teachers often leads to many teachers exiting the profession within 5 years. The focus of this book examines, through personal essays, why I went into this profession and what sustained me through 4 decades. It starts with being fired during my student teaching practicum and ends with me being hired by an Ivy League university as their faculty director of science and teacher education programs.

At first glance, these essays may seem like an unkempt time travel journey as they flow between two careers— one as a high school teacher and the other as a university professor. Or, too specific to offer any pragmatic advice for preservice and teachers just beginning their professional careers. However, I argue that four essential traits—passion, flexibility, building community, and developing intellectual engagement—are needed, regardless of ones' teaching discipline in the practice of teaching. They need to be the rudder that guides them through the uncharted waters they will navigate, and it will ultimately sustain their fire to make a difference in children's lives

The format I offer are personal essays and reflections gleaned and developed from my personal journals written over the years. Each essay is built around these four cornerstones of good teaching. While there are many books written about educational pedagogy as well as methodology, this collection is about why individuals go into teaching and what sustains their passion and fire in the belly to continue.

As true of any profession, there is an associated sea of acronyms and specialized vocabulary that may be unfamiliar to some readers. The appendix includes a short glossary of professional education organizations and terms as well as a methods / pedagogy matrix for designing curriculum. My intended audience includes preservice teachers, beginning teachers, experienced teacher-leaders who coach new teachers, and all those interested in how education happens. Let's roll up our sleeves and get started.

Section 1: Passion

To be or not to be a teacher, that is the question...

"Teaching is impossible, I need to find another career." Dan Bisaccio

That was it. It was just a one-line entry in my journal written six weeks into teaching that first year. I shared that written reflective segue into teaching with my preservice graduate students at an Ivy League college during my final year of teaching—forty years later—as their professor of science education in an Analysis of Student Teaching course. They looked at me in disbelief. I reread and said, "Yes, it's true," as I showed them my forty-year-old journal.

Well, they knew the ending of that story ... I was retiring after forty years in education that year, "graduating" with them onto new beginnings. Thirty years as a high school science teacher followed by the past ten as a professor in science education.

We were six weeks into their student teaching experiences and their newness, aka "grace period," with students had waned and they were gaining experiences in the nuances of how schools operate. Now came the real struggles with reaching all students: homework not being done, classroom management, changes in school schedules due to snow days or fire drills or lockdowns, parent conferences, issues with colleagues, issues with students, English language learners, special education IEPs and how to adapt lessons, etc.

That afternoon they understood that it wasn't just them, teaching is and has been and will continue to be a very challenging profession.

Why do some people choose to teach?

Charismatic teachers do make an impression. Many of my teaching colleagues from the 1970s in the social sciences credit "that teacher" who transformed them into a radical communist for a semester, helping them write their own personal manifesto. English teacher colleagues speak of their transformation into a journalist, poet, or novelist drinking coffee and smoking cigarettes following a course with a beloved English teacher.

For me it was a 6th grade teacher teaching about the anatomy of an atom. Understanding protons, neutrons, electrons … atomic numbers and atomic mass… and isotopes were over the top! Then in 7th grade, I was in a life science "lab." The ultimate. True, I had a crush on my teacher too. Hormones ruled more than gray matter during those turbulent adolescent years, but I stayed true to my course ... science.

Certainly, in college and then in graduate school, I was very fortunate to have professors who taught by using inquiry and observational methods versus straight lecture. It was during my first ecology class that I learned how to read a landscape, which increased my ecological and observational abilities but certainly challenged my focus as a driver on the open highways forever.

* * *

Once we get beyond that initial question, there are some deeper questions that follow: what supports and sustains teachers in their professional lives? How do they develop from a novice teacher to an inspirational and motivational guide for students to become self-advocates, movers and shakers of norms, and lifelong learners? How does an educator reach the diversity one finds in their classrooms?

Although anecdotal stories do not equal data, what follows are my field notes in teaching—often humorous, sometimes heart-wrenching, and hopefully compelling as to why teaching is the world's best profession for some and how one sustains that fire in the belly to teach.

The core of the struggle between "why I want to teach" and the parameters that are both in place in schools as well as put on teachers as they begin are often at odds with why they chose to teach. This leads to almost 40% of newly hired teachers exiting the profession within 5 years. The focus of these essays examines why I went into this profession and what sustained me through four decades. It starts with me being fired during my student teaching practicum and ends with my being hired by an Ivy League university as faculty director of their science education and teacher education program.

To begin this conversation, I start with a "knock, knock" on my office door one recent semester's end.

An Education 900 student came to visit me today. It was the end of the fall semester with exams, papers, presentations done, and grades submitted. He wanted to talk about becoming a science (physics) teacher before heading home for the holiday break.

I asked him why.

He then recounted a conversation he and other Education 900 students were having in a car returning from one of my field trips.

This course was "easy" stated one … that was followed by students thinking and commenting on the past semester. He then added some of the statements that followed …

"We read a book every week, wrote a paper every other week, visited and observed classrooms each week, had two extra field trips, and a 2.5 hr. seminar discussing the book and how it related to what we were observing in classrooms each week."

"And ended with a final 15-page original research paper on classroom interactions between students and teachers based on our observations and seminar discussions."

"I didn't know how to do '*real*' research before this class."

"No, it wasn't easy … it was a course driven by passion, not pressure."

I listened to his story recapping the conversation and appreciated this insight to student thoughts and reflections on this past semester (which will be augmented by the more formal tabulated course evaluations sent to me next month).

He then went on to say that he never thought about education or instruction as "passion," his view of education was about "pressure." His previous experience in education (elementary through college) was all about pressure to do well vs. passion for learning. This was a tipping point for him, and he wanted to share his passion for physics with future students.

This student went on to tell me that he shared this insight with some of his co-concentrators. All stated that they wanted to go into financial management ... as engineers! He also mentioned that he felt becoming a teacher would continue his intellectual engagement. I concurred! At this point in our conversation, I mentioned that 40 years ago, friends tried to discourage me from becoming a teacher as they thought I would become bored. That, I told him, was never a word I would use to describe my many years in this profession. There is so much hope in the future if we continue to give students—early on through college, graduate school—the optimism and thoughtful structures to think about what education is and means.

Student Teaching 101 _
Getting Fired

"You never went to kindergarten and learned
how to follow the rules." MMB, my spouse
and best friend.

Becoming a teacher was a most unexpected accident of circumstance for me.

As a youngster in Queens, NY, there was a lot of urban nature around me. I enjoyed walking on the broken pavement in an area that would soon become a large housing project. The area was a forest of tall cattails towering over my head. I fished for perch in a nearby pond, watched grey squirrels and the occasional rabbit skirt across the uneven paths that I traversed. "Stranger-danger" was decades away from being coined as a phrase to describe a concept that probably existed but wasn't given the newsworthy status it has today. Consequently, my home range was vast to explore each summer day.

One summer, my grandparents, uncle, and aunt asked me to join them on a vacation to Maine. My parents agreed and off I went spending two weeks in a cabin in a real forest of trees. Hours were spent collecting as many frogs as I could and secretly stowing them away in my grandfather's suitcase for me to take home. Yes, as it turned out, not a good decision as evidenced on the day we began packing for home.

Certainly, inspired by this recent nature experience and now at home, I decided to collect birds. I set up a simple box trap with a string attached to a propped stick and baited with bread to catch blue jays. Success! As a nine-year-old, I was so proud of each blue jay that I managed to lure into this simple trap and released them all … perhaps a dozen … in our garage for my dad to see when he returned from work that evening.

Also, not a good decision. Blue jays spending a day in a garage are not happy birds. Dad's reaction to angry birds strafing him as he opened the garage door was like my grandfather's a few weeks before. I will leave it at that.

Experience is the name we give our mistakes. However, these experiences among others led to my curiosity about the natural world and I believe put me on a path to study biology and geology as an undergraduate.

My geology advisor was a nationally well-known science education reformer who had been pushing my thoughts and others on what education was all about. "Bill" was inspirational, intelligent, and to me, the closest person I had ever known to be a true Renaissance person. I was intrigued and began reading the "radical" education reform books of that time. *Teaching as a Subversive Activity*, *Summerhill*, Paulo Freire's timeless book, *Pedagogy of the Oppressed* were a few that began to rough out a teaching identity for myself.

Then, between my junior and senior year, I had the opportunity to teach chemistry and biology for an Upward Bound program in St. Lawrence County, NY. The opportunity also allowed me to be a resident assistant in a dorm for the high school students as well as lead weekend field trips to the Adirondack Mountains. A perfect incubator for my evolving sense of what it means to be a teacher.

The students were either from a nearby Akwesasne (Mohawk) Reservation or rural communities throughout that county. At this point in my undergraduate career, I had already begun getting to know these communities. Beginning in my freshmen year, I volunteered in a campus program known as the Community Development Corps. We worked with families mostly struggling with poverty, alcoholism, sometimes abusive partners, or all the above. We offered tutoring to their children and acted as a conduit for social services, community resource partners, and medical professionals who could provide some much-needed assistance to them.

Upward Bound became a professional segue for me to fuse my passion for science with a developing awareness of social and environmental justice issues. This new lens in viewing the discipline of education through greatly appealed to my growing affinity and identity with environmental social justice.

The completeness of the Upward Bound community experience—supportive small classes, residential dorm life, weekend camping and field trips—fostered the importance of learning as a human experience.

It certainly reinforced teaching science as science is done as my pedagogical mantra.

Mike, a friend and Upward Bound colleague, was teaching in the program as well. He was preparing his students for their NY State history Regents exam. One afternoon as we were discussing our emerging ideas on educational reform, he recounted a factoid that he was supposed to teach: the "discovery" of Hudson Bay. Really? How do you begin to teach Akwesasne children that someone named Henry Hudson discovered their home? Cultural and historical relevance had not yet entered the curricular vernacular or conscience. Yes, change on so many levels were desperately needed.

* * *

At that time, the path to becoming a certified teacher in a small liberal arts college or university required that one completed their core discipline requirements in their major and then enroll in a "professional semester" that included education courses and a student teaching practicum.

My emerging teaching philosophy was all about active student engagement. "To teach science as science is done." Students needed to be scientists ... exploring, using their own questions to guide their learning and for them to construct their newly acquired knowledge. But how does this happen in a classroom?

I was about to find out and what the consequences would be for an earnest neophyte student teacher.

"This is Mr. Bisaccio, he is a student teacher and will be teaching you the next 12 weeks". After that brief introduction, my cooperating teacher left the room for the faculty lounge where he would be during most of my weeks in that school. To be fair, he would come back on unannounced occasions to observe me a few times each week.

Teaching 6 sections of 9th grade earth science—4 "regents", 1 "non-regents general", and 1 "honors regents"—were going to be challenging, exhilarating, and a path to my dream coming to fruition. The classes were homogeneously grouped, a concept that I was not familiar with. Although I went to high school in this state, my experience was in only one of those aforementioned tracks. In retrospect, my early naivete of "tracking" was probably best for all my students. A "general" class was the euphemism for nonacademic or "slow learners." The labels mattered little to me as I designed my lessons.

Creating curriculum where students constructed knowledge versus memorizing content was my ideal that I tried to reach. My early attempts at project-based and inquiry-driven lessons were simple and uninformed by what would become a rich field of educational research in the coming decades. That later research solidified my pedagogical understanding of what I was trying to do with students. Nonetheless, for now, it was allowing my students to "muck about" and follow their questions in their explorations into earth science phenomenon.

And mucking about it was! We made models of glaciers using grape jelly sliding down cardboard mountain troughs, examined how streams modify landscapes with a makeshift stream table that I made. My cooperating teacher would just smile, shake his head, and return to the faculty lounge.

Entering my final weeks of student teaching I was wondering how to create an investigative context for teaching about wind's erosional and depositional characteristics. Here is what emerged:

"Project Sand Dune Formation"—we would investigate and develop the five types of dunes: crescentic, linear, star, dome, and parabolic.

Buckets of sand, hair dryers, and … 6 periods of "mucking about" created an indoor dust storm of sorts. It was the end of the school day when my cooperating teacher peaked into the classroom … this time, he wasn't smiling.

With two weeks left in my student teaching practicum I was called to the principal's office the next morning before the start of school for a meeting with him and my cooperating earth science teacher. I was "fired" and told to leave the school immediately. My cooperating teacher had had enough of my projects and inquiry-based teaching style. What was most difficult for me that morning was the fact that I did not have a chance to say goodbye to my young earth scientists … my student teaching experience felt and was unfinished.

Back on campus, the geology and education departments congratulated me on being resolute regarding my convictions and passion for student inquiry as a pedagogy for learning. However, a dean who was the advisor for "Baker Scholars" was not amused. I had been one of four entering freshmen students who received that scholarship. To this day, I think it was part of a social experiment. As incoming students, we were identified as potential "change makers," entrepreneurs, creators who think outside of the box. As such, we were given a full ride (tuition and housing) and free reign to take whatever courses we chose—no course requirements. We were also told that the foundation would be tracking our future paths. During my meeting with the dean, that "change maker" and "think outside the box" mantra seemed to have some limits that I transgressed. He graphically warned me (literally motioning his hand as if he was cutting his throat) that I was on a "difficult" path unless I learned to compromise my ideals.

I was 21, about to graduate, hoping to find a teaching position, and wondering if that was a good idea.

"Jump, the net will find you."

All you could hear was the soft calming "blurp" of the intersection between paddle with water as Marco and I canoed slowly through the sawgrass marsh. It was hard to imagine that just a few days before, Tropical Hurricane Roxanne was ravaging this nature reserve in Quintana Roo, Mexico. Suddenly, we flushed a snail kite that flew overhead. That instant jolt of energy reminded me that we had been paddling for an hour and I had no idea where we were in this vast marsh. Towering sawgrass and cattails dominated our 360^0 views for the past hour.

"Marco, do you know where we are?" I asked. His calm response: "No worry, we have nothing better to do."

I should have known that he would have a response such as that. A few weeks ago, before departing with 8 high school students to this reserve, another hurricane, Opal, danced over this very region in a very busy tropical hurricane year. Given the reports, I phoned Marco asking about the storm's impact on our proposed trip to this reserve to start a Smithsonian Monitoring and

Assessment Biological Diversity study site. His response: "No worry, we have canoes." I smiled.

Marco, the director of a newly established ecological wildlife reserve, exuded an unperturbed and confident presence. All I needed to do was to translate that essence to the parents of the 8 students that I was taking with me to this reserve that October 1995. As it were, I'd handpicked the 8 students from a larger group of students that I had previously taken with me to Costa Rica the year before. My thought was that I had already established "trust" with those families in bringing their child safely back from the "jungle." Nonetheless, that last evening parent meeting before we departed there were many questions. I did my best answering them even though I had never been to this reserve before and wasn't quite sure what to expect as well. At one point, a parent asked about "seat belts" on the vehicle transporting us to the airport. Intentionally, I droned on and on about the safety of this vehicle, hoping and hoping no one would extend the question to what our transportation was like once we landed in Mexico. That much I knew from my conversation with Marco. He would be there to scoop us up on the back of a cattle truck to take us out to the reserve.

What I did know for sure, was that my 8 students and I were very excited to head off to the El Eden Ecological Reserve and start what would become a 25-year biodiversity project. Over those years, I led several trips per year that included close to 400 students and close to 100 teachers on those biodiversity adventures.

Sometimes the best ideas are hatched on the back of a napkin in unexpected places. This was one of those happenings.

Up until this point, I was leading an annual trip for high school students to tropical forests in Belize or Costa Rica. Additionally, I was teaching—as an adjunct professor—a tropical terrestrial ecology course in Jamaica during my high school winter break. Although the high school trips were wonderful, they lacked the focus of really "doing science" in the field as my college course did. I was looking for an opportunity to change that and that opportunity came while I was attending my wife's 20th high school reunion.

Reunions are by nature a social gathering. Ironically, they can be anything but social for those attending without any common context. Attempts at ice-breaking chitchat is limited. After all, initial forays to engage conversation such as "you look good"; "nice to see you again"; "remember that time …" are absurd conversation starters for the outsider. I credit the emcee of this gathering for being more inclusive. His queries to his classmates included who had the most children and who came the longest distance to attend. That second question grabbed my interest … Bob was the winner of the distance question. He was an entomologist now living in Chiapas, Mexico. My wife knew him as a fellow member of the high school band they had both played for. She seized the opportunity for me to talk with someone who I could relate to on matters other than 20-year-old school gossip.

During our conversation, Bob mentioned that a newly formed ecological reserve in the Yucatán was looking for researchers to start projects there. I was intrigued and talked about my beginning "HabitatNet" biological diversity project. He suggested that I join him at the reserve that following fall. Napkins soon filled with notes, names to contact at the reserve, and potential project ideas as well as promises to keep in touch with one another during the ensuing months. Little did I realize then that this chance meeting would redirect much of my professional career in the coming decades.

Down the road of time and ten years in, I would be hosting an international symposium on biodiversity at the El Eden Reserve for 80 students from 12 countries (More on that adventure in a later essay.).

For now, however, HabitatNet found a field site in the Yucatán that welcomed young student field researchers. It is worth noting that many colleagues often asked me (and perhaps as a reader, you too, share this question) how I was able to get a public school to approve a teacher taking 12 – 15 adolescents to Cancún, Mexico annually?

Passion is contagious. The administration and school board noticed how excited the students were coming back from our first biodiversity adventure in a Yucatán forest. My hope was to sustain and grow this project and needed a strategy. So, in year two, I invited a school board member to join our trip. "Dave" had a forestry degree and welcomed a spot on our roster even though I charged him twice the cost of the trip. That extra funding, I explained, would go toward scholarships for students who did not have the same economic opportunity as others.

During the week, Dave enjoyed the same mosquitoes, mud, scratches, and other normal torments of biodiversity field researchers as the rest of us and he became the best ambassador for HabitatNet. In fact, he advocated for a permanent "scholarship" fund for future students to participate as he continued to regale our Yucatán forest project at each of the monthly school board meetings upon his return that year.

Those initial notes on a napkin, began with a passion to provide authentic field research opportunities for high school students and led to my humble "HabitatNet" project becoming recognized by the Smithsonian Institution's Monitoring and Assessment of Biodiversity program as well as the United Nation's Convention on Biological Diversity.

Why do I include this essay in this collection of reflections and teachable moments? It isn't about starting an international field research project for students. It is about following your passion as an educator in developing new, maybe even outrageous, opportunities for your students.

I met an expat now living in a coastal Mexican village named Goyo (probably a new name too). He drove his 1980s pink Cadillac to Puerto Morelos, Mexico, to start a new chapter in his life. Leading jungle and cenote tours for tourists out of his newly converted "caddy-offroad vehicle" was his newfound profession. I don't know his backstory, but his motto, painted on the side of that unique vehicle was: "Jump and the net will find you." I agree.

Another day at "the office" (or why teach outdoors?)

The conversation is now turning from pandemic to endemic as we enter year three of COVID-19 and how we will live with it as we go forward. A hope that I have is that we do not leave the outside classrooms that many schools have adopted for the indoors. Why did education become an indoor activity to begin with? Perhaps, our outdoor classrooms will become endemic as well. I certainly hope so.

For most of my teaching career, I taught many of my classes outside. Questions from some of my colleagues included "What do you do outside?"; "Are the students just playing?"

Typically, I would respond with "Why should school be an indoor activity?" The context for learning is equally important to the lesson's content. Content isn't irrelevant and, in fact, it gains relevancy when taught in a meaningful context. Teaching outside expands the conception of "lesson plan" to an integrated instructional sequence that translates learning outcomes into problem-solving strategies.

When lessons are taught outside, we are necessarily reminded to connect across boundaries in four key context realms:

- Place and Learning
- Doing and Knowing
- Individual and Group
- Reflection and Action

Those connections lead to links between self, place, and others. Add reflection to this mix and that transforms those experiences into lifelong learning.

Student voice. My journals include correspondence with former high school students over the years that directly speak to this. A few examples follow.

"Hi Dan, I've been meaning to email you for a few years now and figured now is as good a time as any. I want to tell you that I am about to graduate with a PhD in Environmental Science and have been working in land conservation for over 10 years now. Every single time someone asks me how I got into this field I tell them about you and the influence you had on me. Specifically, there was one day in our high school science class when we were studying wildlife outside. I will never forget what you said to the class: "Who cares about this wildlife? If we don't have this habitat they will have nowhere to live." Right then and there I realized I better protect the habitat. And that is exactly what I've done since. I am so passionate about my work. It gets me up early every day, keeps me up late at night, and makes me so happy. I have you to thank for this! I just want to make sure you know. And that you realize the influence you have on kids. Thank you."

"This vacation I was visiting my grandparents in North Carolina. They started talking about birds and I started asking them about it and what birds they were seeing. They were surprised that I was interested and talking to them about this—so was I! It brought back memories of our classwork outside."

A Facebook Identification Request from a past student:

"Dan Bisaccio, I am in Mexico and there is this bug/ moth/hummingbird thing, it's the first time I have seen it, it flies like a hummingbird and feeds on the nectar of flowers, when still it looks like a moth... any idea what this thing is?"

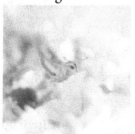

Another former student seeing this post added: "I love that it is ten years since Dan, Dan Bisaccio, was our teacher, and yet he is still our go-to guy for creature identification!"

Dan Bisaccio "Nice photos! Wish I was there—Yes, it is a hummingbird moth also known as a sphinx moth."

Samantha Allen "Thanks to you Dan for starting my enthusiastic interest in this stuff... my excitement continues to this day, 11 years after you took us into the field."

Dan Bisaccio "Thank you ... enjoy your trip!"

"Thinking of you, Dan Bisaccio, as it's Aldo Leopold's birthday today. I remember your assignments from The Sand County Almanac and know it's one of the reasons I value and appreciate environmental writing. You took a bunch of mill town kids and accepted us for who/where we were and helped us see the beauty in ourselves and the natural world around us. So, thank you Mr. B, and happy birthday Mr. Leopold."

Rachel, now a science teacher, messaged me with this…

"Taking students into the field by myself for a weekend crash course in water quality and biodiversity with Headwaters Institute.

My motto this weekend is WWDBD or "What Would Dan Bisaccio Do?"

And …. One last email message:

"Dan!

As I officially ended my undergraduate career this December, I can't help but think back to where my journey started. Rooted in the conservation biology class you taught... I now hold a BS in Environmental Science with a concentration in conservation biology and biodiversity (whoot whoot!). Though, unfortunately, our paths have been kept apart these past years, the interest in the world around us that you helped wedge into me has been able to grow and push me towards a future in which I can hopefully do what I love. I just wanted to write and let you know how much your passion has influenced my education. As I wrap up my independent research this spring and then find my way into the unknown world (before eventually heading to graduate school, I think)

I hope that we can stay in touch! May your enthusiasm never fade."

Certainly, I smile and treasure these messages from past students. All these students and the many others came into my classes with youthful sparks. Certainly, not all of their sparks were about nature or being outside. My challenge, as their teacher, was not to wring out their passion, inquisitiveness, or joy but to get them outside to make connections, gain insights and inspiration from being outside four walls enables. Their insights came from a merger between landscape and mindscape.

It sometimes starts with that little spark from an observation and question: "Hey, Mr. B., I saw a small brown bird and it has wings. What is it?" Or perhaps the most astute observation one student made at the end of a field project: "Biodiversity work is itchy."

At end of those wonderful school days when I taught my classes outside and my boots were covered with mud … and, perhaps, some vegetation was attached to my clothing, a colleague would ask, "What happened to you?" My response was always, "Just another day at the office."

The Irony of Professional Development

The context in which we create and deliver instruction must encompass the richness, complexity, and ambiguity of day-to-day life and worldly situations. Lifelong learners emerge from this stew. Biologists often cite "form follows function" in trying to interpret patterns observed in our natural world. If our function as educators is to assist young learners in becoming lifelong learners, we too must exemplify what it means to be a lifelong learner.

Of course, there are some embedded ironies in all of this. Teachers are asked to differentiate to meet the learning needs of all students yet need to prepare them for standardized statewide proficiency tests. School administrators tout the need for professional development, while offering the "one size, fits all" professional development for their educators. This is more than likely related to budget (it is less expensive to host district-wide "pd" then individualizing the "pd" needed) and a seemingly "efficient" pathway to meet current school mandates with target goals ("√").

In THE COURAGE TO TEACH, Parker Palmer writes: "Good teaching can never be reduced to technique. Good teaching comes from the identity and integrity of the teacher."

Good teaching does start with a teacher's professional sense of self, also known as teacher identity, and technique alone, as Parker states, does not make a good teacher. Effective teaching blends both and not pit as a dichotomy of one versus the other. Good technique will enhance the cognitive framework of your teacher identity.

What is meant by teacher identity?

Teacher professional identity is often defined as the beliefs, values, and commitments an individual holds toward being a teacher. Researchers include five psychological processes involved in the development of a teacher identity: a sense of appreciation, a sense of connectedness, a sense of competence, a sense of commitment, and imagining a future career trajectory.

Another important aspect of teacher identity includes the sense of belonging to the profession. A sense of belonging, coupled with imagining one's own teacher's trajectory evolves over time in a career. It is not hard to understand that a beginning teacher's worldview of this profession is different from a mid to later career teacher's focus. A teacher's identity does affect the classroom environment because the teacher sets the tone and culture of the classroom based on their values, attitudes, and belief system.

Recognizing the different professional needs of teachers as they develop their art and technique of teaching is not complex or need be an added expense to a school's tight budget. Some schools have begun to recognize this and are developing "professional learning communities" where teacher leaders within their school are identified and trained to facilitate meaningful conversations as small groups of educators working on student learning initiatives.

Imagine professional learning communities that focus on what does it take to be a teacher-leader mentoring novice teachers in their schools. Freshly minted novice teachers need the added mentoring during their first several years. Nationally, we lose 40% of year 1-5 teachers. Teacher-leader mentors would reduce this statistic and simultaneously reduce the number of experienced teachers from leaving the profession who need a new professional challenge that utilizes their acquired skills. Win-win.

Imagine a professional learning community of educators within a school discussing: new curriculum initiatives to increase student learning; discussing policy around cell phone use, student tardiness, parent involvement, etc. Teachers know their students, community, and need to share their professional voice and experience in creating any necessary policy versus mandates from above. Educators are the heart and soul of all school communities and need to be respected to contribute to emerging policy needs.

Imagine a professional learning community as a "book club" for teachers. Imagine this! A structured time when educators may leave their grading, phone calls to parents, and lesson planning to instead meet with colleagues to, for this one moment each month, to engage in reading and discussing a thought-provoking book as professionals.

Professional learning communities are just one example of how to impact the professional culture of educators to sustain continued growth in the practice of teaching. Biologists know that healthy community populations need to include genes from outside their local gene pool too. It is important for individual teachers to occasionally attend professional conferences as well.

Attending conferences reminds novice teachers that they are a part of a larger community of professionals engaged in conversation, evolving methods, strategies, and technique, to improve learning in their classroom. Attending conferences for more experienced educators allows them an opportunity to share what they are doing in their classrooms with other. All of this builds a professional culture and camaraderie along the way … the professional journey of teaching.

During those last few classes with my graduate students who are going into teaching, we would discuss strategies for keeping their fires burning. Eat lunch with colleagues who have a similar disposition toward teaching and children versus those who are negative, make room for your own life each day, get outside—go for a run or a walk. Lastly, with the caveat of "do not try this until you have been teaching for at least 10 years" and you now have some time to do this, try getting an adjunct teaching position at a local community college or college. Not so much for supplementing income but for getting back into your love affair with your academic discipline.

It is time to dispense with two cliches: "one size fits all" and "you can't teach an old dog new tricks" when it comes to professional development. Instead, we need to reimagine a tiered approach to ongoing professional development that meets the needs of individual teachers while keeping that fire in the belly burning for why they chose to teach.

Section 2: Flexibility

Look for a White Van

Landing at Hong Kong International Airport after 19 hours of flying I was feeling excited and not exhausted as friends had warned. My department chair asked me to go to China to meet with 30 Chinese educators who would in turn, be visiting our Providence, RI campus in the weeks ahead. The purpose was to assist them with their preparation for their international travel. I enjoy travel, and this would be my first trip to China. Yes, I was very excited!

There was only direction given to me for after clearing immigration and customs: "Look for a white van". Really? I pushed for more detail and once again the response remained concise and clear … look for a white van. Naively, I thought this must be obvious and made a mental note not to worry, a white van will appear.

My next question focused on the expectations of what I was to do while there including the topics for my workshops. The response was equally concise: "Just be you." So, I was off to Hong Kong and then on to Shenzhen, China with a "look for a white van" and "just be you" as my guides.

Flexibility is characterized as the capability to adapt to novel and changing requirements. This trip would become my final exam on defining this noun in practice.

As it turns out, there are a lot of white vans at the Hong Kong International Airport.

"Hello, I am looking for a white van going to Shenzhen, can you help me?" was met with quizzical and incredulous expressions as I traversed the many levels of that airport asking anyone who looked official. Eventually, I met success.

Mystery solved, or so I thought, I was now in a white van with my luggage and feeling confident that I was finally on route to a hotel (and some sleep) in Shenzhen. About one hour later, the driver stopped the van at what seemed to be a boarder crossing. In fact, it was. He took my bag out and placed it on the curb and bluntly stated to me: "Out! Out! This is as far as I go."

This really wasn't what I wanted to hear after now traveling for over 24 hours. I needed sleep and a bed. My initial excitement began to wane as a more fundamental biological need took over.

It seemed to take forever as the Chinese immigration officer reviewed my passport and visa. He used a thermal infrared device to take my body temperature as he questioned me about all my travel to Mexico documented in my passport before getting to the purpose of my trip to Shenzhen. Eventually, he was satisfied and pointed to another curb for me to stand and wait. It wasn't an eternity, but it certainly seemed like one after the hours of travel that landed me on this curb, now a second immigration check and in the dark waiting for what, I did not know. Then, a taxi arrived.

Fumbling through my papers, I produced a paper that listed my hotel name and address, both in English and Chinese, to show the driver. I was off to Shenzhen, again.

Shenzhen was once a small coastal fishing village. Now it is a sprawling Chinese experimental city of 19 million residents. 70,000 residents are teachers in relatively progressive schools testing new pedagogies. I was beyond thrilled to finally reach my hotel, a very modern 30 floor building that indeed had my reservation.

All it took was a plane, white van, and finally a tiny gray taxi to get me to my bed!

Next morning after a little sleep, my hotel room phone rang. My host and translator asked me to produce a 5-day syllabus for my workshops and to meet her at breakfast in 10 minutes. "Just be you" was now a pesky little voice in my head as I fired up my computer and strung together a number of inquiry-based workshops that I have done over the years for my impromptu "syllabus."

* * *

Day 1 was over. I gave two, 3-hour workshops to a group of "elite teachers and principals." I sensed a very strong emphasis on prestige and formality, which are two traits that would test my comfort levels. Teachers and administrators were selected to participate based on their "status" (I am not sure what the criteria was). Afterward, I had dinner with a highly respected principal who informed me that he could have more than one child because of the respect he has as an educational administrator.

My workshops focused on inquiry and constructionist-based strategies used to engage students. The 3-hour workshop was really a 1.5-hour workshop but given the need for translation, it required the extra time. As an opener, I broke the group up into groups of 4 and gave each group 3 sheets of paper and 1 water bottle. The challenge was to build the highest tower that would support the bottle of water.

My translator did a magnificent job translating and even adding clarification to my attempts at humor. This was followed by silence as everyone patiently waited and looked at me. Chinese culture is very polite. I mistook their silence, thinking they waited for me to say, "You may begin," which I did and was dutifully translated. Now, there was a flurry of conversation and finally the translator said to me, "They are waiting for your directions on how to build the tower."

This took several rounds of back-and-forth conversation with me stating I gave all the direction that is needed followed by polite counter-comments that translated to "you have forgotten to give us the directions."

Finally, everyone understood that I would not be giving any more direction and it was now up to them to complete the task.

We laughed a lot during my workshops and during breaks these next few days. During one of my workshops, I asked them to draw an ant. This is a standard activity of mine to focus on how acute observation and sketching translates to understanding concepts and knowledge acquisition. In short, most people know that an ant has three main body parts and six legs. However, many are hard-pressed when it come to know where to place the six legs correctly. This gave birth to my newly adopted name, "Professor Ant." It was easier to pronounce than my actual name, so it persisted through their visit to my campus later that month and even into my second visit to China one year later where I was introduced as Professor Ant to a new group of Chinese educators.

Every lunch and dinner I was invited out with a small group of participants—I was treated like royalty. They had a sign-up sheet for when a group would take me out for a meal. One of the teachers told me that I was the first foreigner she had ever seen in person.

I was a "big boy" and eating everything that was served— which meant lots of interesting biodiversity (both plants and animals crossing my plate—some with eyes looking "right at ya"). And ... I was trying to eat with chopsticks (I used a "spearing technique"). There was one exception to my culinary adventures ... every meal had chicken feet. I drew the line on that and wondered about all of those flocks of free-range "legless" chickens out there.

As the week progressed and then in the following month back on my home campus our cross-cultural collegial relationship developed into friendships. Three of the teachers volunteered to assist me getting back to Hong Kong via a train. I appreciated that. One had a brother who lived in Hong Kong, and we meet for dinner and a tour of his home before they helped me find my hotel. I promised these three new friends a tour and visit to my home to meet my family on one of the weekends they were free while in the USA.

Six weeks later and now back on campus in Providence, the translator of our visiting Chinese delegation sent an email to my department's administrator overseeing their visit. It stated:

"Dear Ann, do you know that Professor Ant is taking three female teachers to his house this weekend?"

Ann roared with laughter as she showed me that email. The issue was not the fact that a male faculty member was taking three females to his home. The issue was that I had not invited the other 27 Chinese educators! The cultural context of language sometimes needs much more clarification and understanding. This international near incident was resolved. My wife was especially glad to learn that we would not be hosting an international slumber party for 30 that weekend. Instead all 30 met my wife and I for a day in the rural community where I live to enjoy a Pumpkin Festival.

"Look for a white van" and "Just be you" were my initial guides when I departed for China. However, they serve as a broad metaphor for the ever-changing landscape in education. Flexibility is a key component of being an educator. Yes, we have that lesson plan in place, but we need to make room for the unexpected, unplanned, and often serendipitous moments when led to those unplanned and memorial learning experiences.

This section will explore those unplanned moments and the value they serve if we pay close attention to them.

Humor helps too. As a new colleague and friend said to me at the end of one of my workshops in Shenzhen, "Humor brightens a dour day."

Teaching on "that day", 9/11

The morning began with my usual flutter of "stuff to do" preparing for a day in the field with my senior biology classes. I was foraging for the needed equipment, data sheets, reviewing a mental checklist all the while sipping a cup of coffee, and being thankful for a beautiful September day.

It was 7:00 AM and little did I realize, that by class time, our world would have changed. It was Tuesday, September 11, 2001.

8:30 AM. Teachers read the eyes and faces as they teach and work with students. I watched my students coming into class that morning trying to understand this horrific event that was still unfolding. Their eyes told me that they had questions … but their questions were still being formulated. They were not alone.

Clearly, the plan for the day, to collect biodiversity data, did not seem appropriate. Everyone needed some time to reflect as well as search for some meaning to what was transpiring and maybe, even construct hope for our future.

After some initial discussion of what was known at that moment that morning, it was clear that a "Plan B" was needed. A plan that would help them sort information and search for hope. We went outside, not with the equipment and data sheets listed on my lesson plan, but with a copy of Annie Dillard's *Pilgrim at Tinker Creek*. They read her essay on "Seeing" in which she describes hiding pennies for people to find:

"There are lots of things to see, unwrapped gifts and free surprises. The world is fairly studded and strewn with pennies cast broadside from a generous hand," Dillard writes.

The students were then tasked with finding a metaphorical "penny" in the forest that brought them unexpected joy. Specifically, the task was to see, observe, and write about something common that often goes unnoticed but brings joy when we take the time to notice it. We would then share our discoveries at the end of class.

Individually and collectively, the "pennies" that were observed, written about, and shared that September morning were priceless. True, our world was changing, and this horrific event would not go away ... our hearts and minds hurt. However, for a few minutes that morning, time was taken to appreciate our world's beautiful gifts as well. Perhaps, trying to regain some perspective.

Maybe it was an unusual writing assignment for a biology class but one that was needed for that class at that time. Flexibility and adapting to a teachable moment build on developing classroom culture as well. The school year was just beginning with many more days to explore this academic discipline but, for now, we needed to share this human experience in the context of our class.

On the Sixth Day, Let There Be STEAM

Summer, 1991. It was the first, and as it turned out, the only joint Soviet-USA Science Educators Conference to ever take place, which was convening at Moscow State University. The National Science Teachers Association organized the event with its science education counterpart in the USSR for a weeklong exchange between science educators. An emerging "glasnost" spirit coupled with "perestroika" policy changes flowed into the education domain as well and provided this unique opportunity.

During the weeklong conference, pedagogical ideas were exchanged but more importantly, collegial relationships developed that transcended the political boundaries between our two nations. During the social gatherings that included meals, there was much discussion of the "perceptions" we had for one another. One Soviet colleague summed it up as "Americans think of Russians as bears while we think that all Americans are joyful." We all learned that there were many more dimensions to that caricature as well as shared human dispositions.

By any means of evaluation, the conference was a success and promises to keep in touch with one another were made and kept. The internet was still by and large, inaccessible, and clunky for follow-up, so snail mail would be the primary means of communication for a few more years. Decades later, the professional development and spirit of cross-cultural connections in the field of education remain a treasured highlight for me.

As the conference concluded, I remained behind with several other American educators for an extended trip to "Leningrad" to visit the city and the Hermitage. By the time we were returning to Moscow, on that late July overnight train, Leningrad was being transformed back to its original namesake, St. Petersburg. We were witness to the dissolution of the Soviet Union and history being made. There was a frenetic optimism despite a chaotic sense of what was occurring all around us. Only a few days before, we were at an end of a conference celebratory dinner hosted by our Soviet educators in the Kremlin. Now, back in our dormitory rooms at Moscow State University, we were wondering how and when we would be able to return home.

When we landed in Moscow two weeks before, our passports were taken from us with the promise they would be given back to us on the day we departed.

Now, as crowds gathered on the streets of Moscow and Soviet tanks were mobilized on those same streets, our NSTA group waited and watched history being made up close. We continued to wonder. Back home, family and friends also wondered as there was no way for us to communicate with them or for them with us. This unscheduled extended stay lasted for several days while the State Department and NSTA officials in Washington D.C. were in communication with our Soviet (or now, Russian) counterparts. Three days later, our visit was concluded, and we were given our passports and air tickets to Helsinki to begin our journey home.

After returning home, the local newspaper ran a story on their area science educator who was there watching this history unfold. The interview included my stories and photographs of this two-week professional conference adventure.

As the new school year was about to begin, I submitted my professional development paperwork for attending and presenting at this historic conference. This is when I discovered school bureaucracies are unencumbered by the thought process as they protect inflexible mandates and policies. The USSR science educators conference did not have the "correct school district forms" needed to validate my participation in that conference.

Imagine that. Consequently, I was denied professional development credit.

Not to be deterred, this inflexibility inspired me to be mischievous. After my presentation in Moscow, a Soviet colleague gave me a gift ... a wooden physics puzzle with the directions written in Cyrillic. I xeroxed the directions and asked a friend to sign it "Boris Badenov," which I then resubmitted to the school administrative unit as validation of attendance. My professional development hours were now approved. My best guess is that the person reviewing my paperwork could not read Cyrillic and assumed it was, in fact, "district language for conference verification."

The paradox of a flip-flopping flexibility-inflexibility paradigm in many schools is striking. Teachers are regularly expected to change or modify lesson plans with regularity making room for spontaneous mandated fire drills, intruder in the building drills, as well as special administrative assemblies. Reasons that include the need for regular safety practice and worthwhile special all-community events are valid and understood. However, there is no room for flexibility when it comes to adapting school policy for novel and often worthwhile special circumstances such as professional development opportunities for teachers, curriculum innovations that may require some changes in the daily schedule, or even field trips for students. A one-sided top-down approach toward "flexibility" limits the scope of creativity as well as fostering school ownership for teachers and students who are important stakeholders as stated in most school mission statements. It is indeed a paradox that persists but must change.

Fast-forward.

Recently, I have had the opportunity to work with a public elementary school that redefined its mission to a be a STEAM school. The administration asked me to work with students and faculty on STEAM-based curriculum projects to engage students with inquiry tasks and engineering practices. Teachers would submit curriculum topics to me, and we would work together on developing lesson plans to engage students with cross-disciplinary STEAM-infused projects that would be co-taught by us. Soon, our co-planning was complete, and it was time to put into action the lessons with students … or so I thought.

"We're on a six-day schedule and STEAM is only taught on the sixth day" was the only news given to my teaching colleagues by their principal. The teachers were truly excited to share their work, their new curriculum, with their principal. Instead of applauding them for the innovative work they were eager to share with their young scientist-artist (remember, a STEAM-based school community) students, her faculty left her office deflated. It would need to wait until the 6th day of their schedule rotation to begin, with follow-up work by the students every 6 school days to follow. How do you get students to sustain interest, develop scientific / artistic rigor with 5 days in between engagement with their work?

Intentional guiding policies—including discipline policies—need to replace the statically outlived ones for schools to innovate and succeed. Guiding policies must be simple and actively call for reflection, elaboration, and discussion. This is the zone where learning not only happens for all (students, teachers, and administrators) but enables learning. What do I mean by this?

School communities often have "no lists" that grow as societal boundaries change, technology (such as cell phone use) advances, and funding decreases. Examples for revisiting static policies abound. Ever-increasing and diverse online professional development possibilities (courses, workshops, learning community blogs) may fill a great need for rural schools or schools without elaborate funding for ongoing professional development.

Cell phone use is probably the most contested and argued policy in school communities today. School policies regarding both discipline and procedural matters such as implementing new curriculum, technology integration, engaging other forms of professional development require ongoing reflection and discussion as to how it may provide opportunity.

What if schools had just two rules that guide policy and discipline: 1. respect oneselfs' right to learn and, 2. respect others' rights to learn?

Both of these simply stated "rules" seek and call for dialogue that would reflect intent, deeper understanding of what the issue is, and buy-in by school community members. Policies would not become static but instead reflect new understandings and opportunity, thereby being intentional. Perhaps then, on the seventh day, discussion, flexibility, and adaptation would create a human learning community that is the focus of people's lives.

A Clean Stall Means a Dead Horse:

The Importance of Making Mistakes

Science starts with wondering ... and wonder starts with a question. We are a curious species and often playful—especially as children. I am convinced that when we combine our curiosity with playfulness, we are destined to make great discoveries. We become informed along the way by making mistakes... in fact, I am certain that an expert is someone who has made every mistake once and continues.

As a child, I was fascinated by the inventor Thomas Edison. I read biography after biography on his life. It took him 6,000 tries to find the perfect filament for a light bulb. That translates to 5,999 mistakes.

"Before I got through," he recalled, "I tested no fewer than 6,000 vegetable growths, and ransacked the world for the most suitable filament material."

"The electric light has caused me the greatest amount of study and has required the most elaborate experiments," he wrote. "I was never myself discouraged or inclined to be hopeless of success. I cannot say the same for all my associates."

"Genius is one percent inspiration and ninety-nine percent perspiration."

Discovery and wisdom come from the experience of failure and persistence… following a "hunch."

One of the best pieces of advice / wisdom I ever received came from a dairy farmer while I was an undergraduate geology student working on my senior research thesis mapping glacial erratics in northern New York State. On my research days, I would drive to rural farms and ask the owners for permission to walk about their fields and take samples of rock. All agreed, and they would often joke that I should take as much rock as possible. One morning while asking for permission, "Robert" asked me if he could accompany me. Of course, I said yes … anxious to have human company while in the field where I usually just talked to rocks.

He was very curious about my work and the "detailed" notes I was taking in my field journal as we walked his property. At one point, he asked to look at my field notes.

I said yes … but apologetically added that my notes were "messy" not only in a left-hand writer's sort of way but also in ideas and questions. I didn't have a clean idea on what the landscape was telling me yet.

His response:

"A clean stall means a dead horse." A perfect anecdote! We need to follow our inquisitiveness and wonder … false starts … blunders, messes, all give rise to great stories later and keeps our humanness's need to explore and "muck about" alive. His wisdom was born from his own experience with his life's work … and assisted me to understand that if it is messy … it is alive and well.

I went on to understand (thanks to his wisdom) that landscapes are a language and are rich in human anecdotes and metaphors as well. Acquiring language and real knowledge takes steps, mistakes, laughter, thought and reflection … and next steps. So true is all learning.

If it is *worth* doing, it is worth doing … *even poorly*. We need to let our wonder and questions go forward and not be hampered by "getting it perfect" on the first run.

This is so true when we think about ways of how we need to engage children with their journey on becoming "experts." Since mapping glacial erratics, I spent forty years teaching science ... really guiding ... high school students and "teaching/guiding future science teachers."

When I was teaching my high school students, I wanted them, more than anything, to learn science as science is done. This meant being inquisitive ... to follow an idea ... and to investigate. My mantra was "even no data is data" ... what did we learn? What do we need to do next? And encourage them to revise their question ... develop a new way (procedure) to continue, because we just found out something important ... even if it was wrong. We are on our way to understanding.

I know that this is in stark contrast to the current national USA mandates of "No Child Left Behind" and the National Standards "Core Curriculum" movement. Yet, I believe that true curriculum reform needs to be messy. Teachers—who are professionals—need "to muck about" and develop the curriculum that isn't always perfect but allows children to be engaged with the questions and issues in that discipline that allows them to become "expert" in the literacy that defines that discipline (vs. hoping that "b" is the true answer defined by someone else).

"No Child Left Behind" and "The Common Core Curriculum" are all too simplistic attempts that devalue what it means to be human. We are an inquisitive species that enjoys intellectual challenge and playfulness. We should not devalue being "wrong" on the way to engaging inquisitiveness and playfulness. Great teaching allows ... even expects / anticipates wrong answers and then guides students to better questions and ways to answer them.

Perhaps we need to change the way we assess both students and schools so that it matches our humanness— to be creative and explore our wonders.

I am not against correct answers. Answers do not dispel wonder but reinforce it. Answers lead to even greater questions and wonder if given a chance. However, answers should not be a conversation stopper.

Education reform does not need simplistic questions followed by all too simple data analysis to judge ... but better questions followed by discussion and new attempts to help guide and revise great teaching and learning. Perhaps, we should explore looking at how we develop professional learning communities in schools— involving our teachers, students, and their communities as trusted partners in developing rich, vibrant, and rigorous learning opportunities for their communities. We should expect and anticipate mistakes AND take solace in that "mistakes" show we are on the road to becoming knowledgeable as long as we use them to reflect and make change as we go and not just "judge" a mistake as final. They are beginnings to become expert.

Just read the biographies of Thomas Edison, Marie Curie, Albert Einstein, Rosalind Franklin, and Rachael Carson for an insight to what worked for them in their journeys as young students to adults that gave their voices to new ideas and yes, answers and questions … for humanity and our greater planet.

Section 3: Community Building

The Ambush

"You popped into my mind because ED 900 was my favorite class I've taken so far at Brown. It was an environment conducive to getting to know everyone (students and professor) in the class, and not just on a superficial level, but also in terms of how they function, formulate their thoughts, their passions, their styles of learning, and my favorite, their beliefs and moral values. As you could probably tell, I was not a huge talker due to my introverted personality, but I found that I could participate through the writing assignments. That was so important to me; I had never thought about implicit participation, but only explicit participation that involved talking. Writing, even when reflecting on the readings, was my way of actively engaging in the conversation and contributing the thoughts that I hadn't necessarily verbalized during class. I honestly didn't think I would enjoy putting together my final project as much as I did and remembered how much I truly enjoyed putting together my own little 'project' and coming to conclusions that I myself had deduced. It was MY work for once, and not work I was doing for a grade or my parents or someone else, entirely MINE. And that was such a wonderful feeling, to know that even though this wasn't a big deal where I implemented variables and all, the work was ultimately for my own understanding and learning." E. S.   Ed 900 Fall, 2014

Sure, I was very pleased and smiling when I received this email from a former student. Is there any teacher who would not be? She went on to tell me that she was applying for a summer research project. More smiles.

Ed 900 was a weekly field seminar that I was most fortunate to be assigned to teach. It involved examining current classroom practices as well as the challenges in teaching through readings and actual classroom visits in area schools. Those weekly visits grounded our class discussions. Every seminar focused on an "essential question":

- What are the purposes of schools?
- How do these purposes influence teaching and learning?
- What happens in classrooms?
- How does the culture of classrooms and schools influence student learning?
- How might schools and classrooms be changed to make them more effective?

In each class I tried to model a different teaching methodology as well.

For example, in one seminar contrasting teaching methodologies, we would discuss books written by Ted Sizer and E. D. Hirsch. In that class, I would use a "consenso-ogram" model in which, using sticky notes, students would identify where they stood on the Sizer vs. Hirsch teaching style continuum. This gave us somewhat anonymous individual "peer data" on where each individual stood as well as a picture of our classroom community. We would stand back and see the continuum, which was a visual reminder of our need to be respectful of one another's opinion.

Students also completed two short topic papers:

1. "An Analysis of Good Teaching Practice"

Look back at "the best teacher" you ever had. Consider: What made him or her good? Are these characteristics found in all "the best" teachers? What can you learn about effective teaching from the way your own best teacher taught? Consider some of the characteristics discussed in *The Elements of Teaching*. How did your "best teacher" exhibit any of these?

and

    2. "Classroom Interactions"

Classrooms are filled with interactions, far more than an observer can focus on. Becoming an effective classroom observer requires the development of a set of skills to enable you to see and hear those interactions that are of particular interest to you and potentially of significant importance in the learning that is occurring. In this paper you are to write about some specific interactions that you have focused on in your early observations. You must include in your paper descriptions of events and incidents and related dialogue.

These two topic papers led to a field research project paper and presentation given in our final class together.

A consistent observation that I made each time that I taught this class was a particular aha moment my undergraduate students reached. Usually in their third week of classroom observations, they picked up on the fact that all students did not learn they same way they had. Learning styles differed from one student to another. They reached a key realization in the art and practice of teaching.

For many of my undergraduate students, this was their first foray into "field research." I would pose simple questions for them to observe, record, and discuss as a primer for their own eventual project.

For example, I would ask, "What does classroom participation look like?" My use of the word "look" was intentional. Often, we think participation only involves sound—voices responding to a question. I suspect that most teachers hope for 100% student participation each class. In Educ 900, I would often model ways in which you would get that 100% participation without asking for students to raise their hand responding to a question or adding a comment to our discussion. Methods such as using a "response-chain," "turn and talk," "sketching" a concept or dilemma, making an "experience map" are a few such examples in which 100% of your students participate without raising their hand or speaking to the larger class.

All of this is about building community in your classroom. I argue that this is the first and most important step in developing a successful learning environment for the semester or the year if it is a yearlong class.

Classroom culture: setting expectations that you have for your students, your students setting expectations for you, their teacher, and expectations for everyone to be respectful of one and other and "place." I would encourage my graduate students in their pre-profession methods class to develop a lesson plan around "creating a classroom manifesto" encouraging their students to give voice to that classroom document. And … post it! Refer to it when things take a slide.

Of course, building community starts early and with learning your students' names.

Learning names poses more of a challenge in some classes than other. The most challenging class for me to build community within was an introduction to geology course that I taught at another college. Each semester, I would have between 100 – 140 students taking this class. Unlike my Educ 900 seminar meeting once per week, Perspectives of the Earth met twice a week for 1.5 hours. Still, getting to know your students in such a large lecture-style format was a challenge.

Originally, I developed "the ambush" for my large lecture class but found it was also an effective way to begin my smaller seminars as well. Here is how it works. Toward the end of my first class meeting with students, I would hand out a 3 x 4 index card to each student. Probably, most were expecting me to ask them to list "the data" about themselves: What name would you like me to use when I refer to you? Contact information? Why are you taking this class?

Instead, I would ask them to "ambush me" sometime between the end of class and our next class meeting and have a 3-minute conversation about an unusual fact or characteristic they would like to share with me listed on that card. The ambush could occur if they saw me out for coffee, in my office, or just sitting outside. Inevitably, that "3-minute" conversation was memorable. I not only learned their name but something about them. That conversation began our academic journey together and endured. You quickly learn the names and something about each person who ambushed you.

As I write this, I am reminded of a student who was into origami and fashioned that index card into a beautiful bird, another student told me how she purchased one of the books for my class "used" and found a $20 bill in it, and another who was into gardening, gave me a small pumpkin he grew. That pumpkin remained in my office all semester as well as the stories and names of each of the students. As odd and unlikely as it sounds, building community starts with an ambush.

To Muck About & Create a Community of Scientists in Your Classroom:

A Three-Tier Approach in Developing Student Field Research Skills and Knowledge

Often, my classes and writing start with a story. You as a savvy reader and educator know why … to cast "the hook."

Here comes my hook and you may wonder, "Why I am starting a piece on how to get your students outside conducting field research with a misadventure?" (Possibly a second hook?) Read on …

Brad is a student in my conservation biology class. He is also the starting quarterback on our school's football team. One week, due to an unfortunate encounter with ground wasps in my class, Brad was sidelined. His coach understandably and clearly upset, asked what had happened. Brad's response: "I am taking full contact biology with Mr. B."

Full contact science is messy, and as educators, we always need to first prepare for the safety of our students whether in the lab or out in the field. Certainly, the outdoor lesson plan includes variables that are sometimes hidden and therefore require even more preparation to ensure safety for our students as best we can. This is paramount and sometimes, even with utmost planning, encounters such as Brad's, happen.

Doing "real science" is not as straightforward as it is sometimes depicted. Hypotheses often fail, experiments need to be tweaked, (and in the case of field biology) the wildlife you are hoping to observe don't show up during class time, and you as well as your boots get muddy (figuratively and literally) as you muck about along the way doing your best to extract insights into our complicated world.

So why bother to take that extra effort in creating field experiences for our students?

To gain insight into answering this question, I offer the general response I receive from a similar question posed to my students after a field experience is completed: "Was this experience of value to you as a learner and person?" Inevitably, they respond that the field experience was both a challenge and fun. I take exception to their choice of word, fun. What I observe when I see them outside is joy. There is a difference.

Outdoor educational activities will "Ignite a smile and spark epiphanies" writes environmental science student, Julianna Fujii (Fujii, 2020). However, she astutely observes we need to go beyond the quick smiles and epiphanies to foster transcendent behavior with more sophisticated and critical outlooks. A fun activity is welcomed and needed but often translates to a momentary synaptic experience while joy connotes a more lasting presence in our minds and hopefully leads to future more scientifically literate positions and actions.

The joy that I observe is based on the shared participation in the creation of new knowledge as well as skill development between students and between students and teacher. Collectively, students are making meaning through discovery. In other words, learning science by doing science. The key is mutual and equal participation. Every question posed, every mistake made is honest and valued along the way. Yes, mucking about is an effective teaching strategy.

Effective teaching (Terenzini, 2020) is framed by the challenge of doing fieldwork, which encourages active real-world learning and promotes reflection. In short, the outdoor lessons become personally meaningful and thereby potentially transformative.

Ultimately, my goal is for students to become a "community of scientists" in my classes. To begin this pedagogical trek, I ask my students two questions before we ever go out to the field:

1. What does it mean to be a scientist?
2. What do scientists do?

Then, at the end of each of our days in the field, they are asked to reflect on their prior response to those questions and jot down some personal notes on how they were scientists that class, that day.

Reacquainting adolescents to their own natural inquisitiveness is my first priority before moving on to the heady substance of developing a field research project. Uncovering that latent natural curiosity is always my first challenge since many of my students have long since explored and mucked around outside as young children.

Over the years, I have devised a 3-tier pedagogical focus, using guiding questions, that takes students from more astute observers of nature to field researchers conducting research.

Tier 1: Rekindling inner curiosity about nature and our surroundings.

Overarching question—What can be observed and tallied?

This is all about providing intrigue while challenging my students to see patterns in the apparent chaos of what they may be initially observing. A "sit spot" is a useful activity to start this process for students' initial exposure to what is around them as it develops awareness and appreciation for the surrounding biological diversity and complexity. This also reminds them to tune in all or most of their senses while tuning out potential distractors (no cell phones during this activity).

My follow up activity directs them to find an ant and to follow it for 20 minutes while jotting down some questions about what they observe. Those are my only directions to this field exercise and starts a research cycle.

Inevitably, my students always come back with questions and surprising observations. Many never realized that there is more than one type of ant. We share our observations and questions as a community of scientists. Small groups are formed to develop a way to answer a question and a research cycle has come about. An observational question is now turned into a hypothesis.

The overarching question for Tier 1 fieldwork is, *what can be observed and tallied?*

Students revisit their hypothesis and begin to develop a plan that includes the types of evidence they need and how the evidence may be tallied as data moving their field experience to tier 2.

Tier 2: A graduated constructivist approach.

Overarching questions—What do you tally? And how do you tally?

As a high school teacher, I was fortunate to teach in two public schools that were members of the Coalition of Essential Schools (CES). The late Ted Sizer, a brilliant educational reformer and founder of CES often visited my science classes in both schools. Following his observation of my classes, we would discuss the 10 Principles of CES in relation to his observations. One principle being "student as worker, teacher as coach" (CES website). Ted enjoyed critically thoughtful conversations about student learning and on one such occasion, I asked him.

"Isn't 'student as worker, teacher as coach' really 'student as worker teacher as manipulator'?"

My intended use of the word "manipulator" was a nonpejorative use of the word to get at the understanding teachers have an academic background that cannot be ignored. In fact, teachers should use their academic background to help create contexts for learning. Those contexts develop into essential questions or stories to engage students. My teaching mantra has always been "content follows context."

Ted, a master of the English language, encouraged me to think in terms of guide vs. manipulator. I agreed.

The tier-2 field experiences are focused on guiding students—a constructionist view that is graduated. Teacher as guide dissolves into fully student directed inquiry over time.

Demonstration of field techniques gathering data, give students the background and experience to answer: what do you tally and how do you tally observations made in the field? In my field courses, I would introduce students to field techniques that examine how we measure biological diversity. Students set up 20 meter by 20 meter study quadrats where they would first identify and measure the diameter at breast height (DBH) of each tree in their study plots. Canopy density would be measured as well. All in all, the data compiled begins to tell the successional history of this habitat. Meanwhile, concurrent studies include Berlese funnel insect traps and bird behavioral observations using a typical ornithological ethnogram.

Humans are by nature curious. As students put field techniques into practice collecting data they are also observing and developing questions about what they see.

Tier 3: A research project is born: drawing conclusions as a community of scientists.

Overarching question: What story is being told by your tally (data)?

Generating their own questions will be new to most students so they will need encouragement and scaffolding. By modeling the questioning process and encouraging student discourse through tier one and two activities, you guide and mentor student actions, interactions, and thought processes. Students will ask questions in an environment where inquiry is not only accepted but fostered.

At this point, each student has rediscovered and honed their observation skills, learned how to measure observations by using specific tools, techniques, and protocols. They are ready to ask and research a question they have authored.

Teaching Tip: How do I keep track of all my students during tier 3? Each student or student group is given a Post-it sticky that they affix to our class poster of the research cycle. After each class, they move their sticky note to where they are in the cycle. This serves two purposes; one, it requires students to self-assess where they are in their research and two, it gives me a class-wide visual to see if an individual, or group, is stuck and may need my quick attention.

Tier three is all about students conducting their research and reviewing their tallies (data) to see what, if any, story, or stories are being told. This culminates with a "scientific poster session" in which the student-scientists present their work to the class.

Teaching Tip: Some students, by the time they are juniors or seniors in high school, may have learned that a final "poster" is all about glitz. Consequently, I try to change that mindset from glitz to substance by providing each student with a manila file folder and a format.

Is it worth the time and effort to take this approach to learning? I think so.

"In the beginning of the year, I hated nature. This course has made me love nature. Last night I was driving home and heard peepers. I have heard them forever but never paid attention to them. So, I pulled over and rolled down my window and listened", Sarah, a former student. (Bisaccio, student journal notes, 05/20/2007).

As difficult as it was for Brad to miss that game, he confided in me that it was worth it after he presented his research project during our poster session that fall. He was a proud member of a community of student-scientists discussing their research.

End Notes

Bisaccio, Daniel. Personal Notes, May, 5, 2007

Fujii, Juliana (2020). Green Teacher, #123, Nature's Powers to Transform Habits, 11-13

Terenzini, Patrick (2020) Rethinking Effective Student Learning Experiences, Inside Higher Ed, July 29, 2020

Common Principles, Coalition of Essential Schools website, http://essentialschools.org/common-principles/November, 2020

Xavier drew a masterpiece and Julia is a scientist

You will find improbable scholars and artists in your classroom if you really look and come to know your students.

As I was setting up for a lesson on "shapes found in nature" and chitchatting with the teacher I noticed one particular student. I began to wonder about this child: why was he so apart from the other students? Why was there a frown on his face so early in the morning? What is his story?

He would have been easy to overlook given that the other children were all curious and excited to have a guest ... "me" ... enter their 2nd grade classroom on this snowy New Hampshire day. There was a dark cloud over his head. You sensed it if you were present and noticed.

My lesson began. Bubbles! I began blowing bubbles and asking the students to be scientists and really look at the bubbles and observe everything about them. "Yes, you can pop them but also look and see something that you can say about them." They giggled, popped some, and observed others.

We discussed what they observed, and I then asked them additional questions: what color or colors did you see? What shape were the bubbles? Were there any triangular bubbles? They laughed. Why not?

This led to talking about eggs and then to some crystals that I brought along for them to observe. We then drew imaginary lines down the middle of ourselves and explored symmetry.

My short lesson was only 1 hour so we moved onto drawing a feather to explore bilateral symmetry.

That particular student who caught my initial attention as I was setting up had a name, Xavier. His early frown now turned to a scowl. He was frustrated with trying to draw an elongated "squished" circle as I described it while I modeled sketching one on the classroom whiteboard. I heard him say softly, "I can't draw." That statement brought me to him, and I quietly went over and asked if I could help. He didn't verbalize a response, just nodded his head yes. So, I took his hand and we both drew a "squished" elongated circle together. I then asked him to draw a line down the middle … he did. "Look, you have the beginning of a feather!" He agreed and even had a small smile that began to erase that frown. Now he was hooked, gaining confidence, and wanted to add some detail to his work. I made some suggestions about adding lines to both sides of the line he drew down the middle of his feather ... he did. He began to see a creation that was his ... a recognizable and beautiful feather. Xavier became an artist.

Another elementary school, another model lesson. This time I would be working with a mixed 5th-6th grade class for two consecutive days. The topic was biological diversity. Certainly, I wanted my activities and explorations to engage my young scientists. More importantly, I wanted them to think and behave as scientists. So, I began by asking them what does a scientist do? Emphasis on the "do." I transcribed their responses on the whiteboard. Then, as a follow-up question, I asked, what skills do scientists use in their work as scientists? Those responses were added to their previously generated list before going outside.

We began our fieldwork exploring their school grounds to make some meaning of what biological diversity is. After a while, I casually mentioned to all that they were very good observers and were noticing the biodiversity around them. There was no need to remind them that observing was one of the characteristics they had listed.

This led to me asking them about another characteristic they had mentioned: measuring. How would you measure biological diversity?

We then went on to examining some of the measuring tools that I brought along with me. All enjoyed the canopy densitometer and commented that is was like a submarine periscope. A few were thrilled to learn that scientists take short cuts. The "DBH (diameter at breast height) tape" had already done the math converting tree circumferences into diameters. All were enjoying the simple fact that we were outside.

My work that morning was coming to a close. We were back inside their classroom to debrief our initial exploration of biological diversity. I used the following question: how were you like a scientist today? Now, the students used their list of traits that they had generated a few hours before to apply toward themselves. They were indeed scientists.

Next morning as I came into their classroom, Julia greeted me with, "Hi Mr. B., you know, I dig holes." She went on to show me that she had found an old-fashioned home electrical fuse in a hole she had recently dug. As I was examining it, she then asked, "Why is the dirt different here?" Not sure why she asked that question,

I asked her to explain what she meant. She went on to say that she recently moved to this area. At her former home in North Carolina the dirt was yellow, yet here, it was brownish black. A very astute observation that was followed by a question, why? Julia was genuinely intrigued by her observation and discovery that now led to a more complex question. She wanted to more deeply and fully understand this difference in soils. That is scholarship, that is being a scientist.

Taking time to listen and interact with students is critical not just for student learning to take place but also encouraging ongoing personal scholarship. She owned that question that came from her own personal observations. As her teacher that morning, I was privileged that she let me enter her world for making meaning. It was now incumbent upon me to guide her to her next step as a young scientist.

This type of student–teacher dialogue does not happen every day or with every student in our classrooms. When it does, we need to honor it and actively try to make more opportunities for these "serendipitous" conversations to occur. Our classroom communities grow student by student.

All Children Smile in the Same Language

It was an unexpected comment, uttered by me, to a spontaneous conversation at an international airport's luggage carousel.

Glancing at my watch, while the luggage began to finally make its circular route, hoping I had enough time to make it through Customs and Immigration before connecting to my flight home. We arrived late. Nearby paced another passenger, probably with a similar concern in mind.

He looked at me and asked, "Vacation?" No, I had responded and added that I was teaching a tropical terrestrial ecology course. "How about you?"

His reply startled me. "Business. Are you one of those environmental nuts?"

My response, at first, was educative as I talked about the value of biological diversity for all of us. No, not a "nut," but someone concerned about the future of all species. He took my response as an opening salvo to unleash his rhetoric against environmentalists "saving owls" and all things green. Our conversation continued and I tried to highlight a few of the human benefits of saving biodiversity: foods, medicines, climate regulation. Clearly, he was not the type that could be swayed by aesthetics or any transcendental philosophical arguments. He was all business, so my tact was talking about the "cost-benefits" of conserving biodiversity.

Our conversation was not going well as he smiled, smirked, and added sarcastic comments to all my points. So finally, I asked him, "Do you have any children?" He answered, yes.

"Without biodiversity, they are fucked" was my final response.

* * *

Let's just say I did not score high marks for diplomacy or community building that day. However, that interaction haunted me. I find it incomprehensible that anyone, including that businessperson I met that day, wakes up in the morning and with their first sip coffee contemplate how they are going to exterminate a species or habitat that day. No one is callous enough to willfully want to cause an extinction. Still, extinction and the loss of biodiversity occurs. Ultimately, it is about the choices we make each day and understanding the connections between our choices and impact of those choices that matter. Education plays a key role in making sense of those understandings and ultimately our personal choices.

All of this was playing through my head as I was shopping for face paint, bubble gum, crayons, and paper in a Mexican market before I was due at a local radio station for an interview later that morning. In two days and over the course of the next two weeks, I would be hosting close to 80 international high school students and their teachers at the El Eden Ecological Reserve for a Youth Symposium on Biodiversity. Marco, the Director of El Eden, arranged for the radio interview that was to set the stage for giving voice to children about their future.

A year before this morning's shopping trip, Marco and I were enjoying a morning coffee at the reserve where I had been taking small teams of students and teachers to conduct biological diversity research. I sleepily suggested that we host an international group of young students at the reserve to discuss why biodiversity matters to their future. Marco said, "Sure". I think that I choked on my next sip of coffee, simultaneously realizing, and not fully realizing what I had just proposed. In my mind's eye, I could see my wife and hear her telling me not to come home with any new ideas for projects. With always a knowing smile, that was her mantra before I would leave for a conference or field project.

This idea, to host an international youth symposium at the reserve, did come to fruition. The reserve had a human "carrying capacity" for 20, so I put a call out for students on a website for small student teams to apply for a spot. Each accepted team would collaboratively work on a document that would eventually be sent to world leaders and the United Nations Convention on Biological Diversity on why conserving biological diversity was important to their future. Together, we would also continue a biodiversity research project at the reserve as well. Simple enough.

The reserve is completely off the grid without cell phone or internet service. So, I thought that each of the accepted teams would provide an after-dinner informal talk as a form of entertainment. Each team would be responsible for giving a short presentation to the entire group attending on a biodiversity project they are working on in their home country. Biodiversity research in the morning, work on drafting a document in the afternoon, and evening team talks to round out the day … that was my lesson plan.

Word did spread from one website to another, from one school to another and within two months I had 80 students, from 9 different nations, apply for the 20-person maximum symposium. Their application essays were compelling so all 80 were accepted. That was the easy part, now came the logistics.

How do we transport, house, and feed 80 people at the reserve? How many different languages will be spoken and how do we address that? What about funding? Some will need visas to enter Mexico and will need support to get those visas.

Those and several other challenging logistics were looming but were just that … logistics to be figured out. The more elegant and core challenge was how to build a community quickly among these 80 adolescents?

This called for expertise beyond any that I had. Fortunately, that expert needed was a friend and colleague. Kurt was an English teacher at the high school I taught at was a co-founder of The Arts Literacy Project at Brown University. Integrating the various art forms with other academic disciplines was his forte. He and I had previously worked together presenting professional summer institutes for teachers and I saw the power and genius of his work building community among our participants.

When I described the project to Kurt, he responded, like Marco: "Sure." A project of this scope needed individuals who were not encumbered by "the logistics" but instead saw the potential for creating a memorable community committed to a worthwhile action.

Shopping at the market was now complete. I had the materials we would use to engage and build community before any biodiversity research or writing of a "youth accord" were to begin.

Soon after the waves of students arrived at the reserve on the back of a cattle truck, Kurt led a series of community building exercises that brought smiles, laughter, and the initial beginnings of friendships among the students. Overall, the students spoke six different languages. However, all could speak either Spanish or English so we did our work together with students translating those two languages for one another each day. My guidance on language differences came from a poster I once saw hanging in an urban elementary school: "Children smile in all languages." Learning should not only be meaningful but joyful in the process as well.

Their work as young field scientists and global policy influencers began in earnest.

Biodiversity research was conducted each morning with the students responding to the following prompt in the afternoon for discussion: what would you tell world leaders about why saving biodiversity is important to you as future leaders on this planet. Those evening team talks turned out to be much more than just after-dinner entertainment. A takeaway from those evening talks was each student knowing that they had kindred spirits across the globe.

A draft document was produced by the end of the two weeks. More online work and collaboration followed once the students returned home. By Earth Day that year, it was completed and sent off to several world leaders as well as to the United Nations Convention on Biological Diversity.

Global Biodiversity Day is celebrated on May 22–the birthdate of Karl von Linnaeus who originated our species taxonomic classification system. On that date, one year following the students' submission to the United Nations, student participants were invited to the UN Convention on Biological Diversity's headquarters in Montreal, Canada, to read and record their accord into the official proceedings of the day.

It all starts with building a community. Many of those students continue to keep in touch with one today.

* * *

HabitatNet International Biodiversity Symposium for Youth

To: The United Nations General Assembly, New York, NY USA

During a two week period in January, 2005, seventy-three courageous and committed high school students, representing nine nations from around the world, came together for the FIRST "Youth Symposium For Biodiversity".

This grass-roots project was organized and coordinated by HabitatNet (Souhegan High School – Amherst, NH), El Eden Ecological Reserve (Quintana Roo, Mexico), and Amigos de Sian Ka'an (Quintana Roo, Mexico) and held at the El Eden Ecological Reserve.

Students attending the Global Symposium for Youth on Biodiversity submitted project abstracts regarding the conservation work they are doing at their home sites. All worthy projects were accepted, and funding was found for all to attend.

During the two-week period, these high school students overcame language and cultural differences while collaboratively writing a "Youth Accord On Biodiversity Conservation". Conserving global biodiversity was their central theme. All of the students presented the work they are doing at their home sites to the other students (and began developing a network of "kindred spirits" of youthful peers concerned about their collective future and beyond), collaborated on a biodiversity conservation project at the El Eden Ecological Reserve, and put their collective voices to print! Their voices follow.

Through Global collaboration on biodiversity conservation, our cultural and biological future is ensured.

Dan Bisaccio,

Project Director - HabitatNet @ Souhegan High School, Amherst, New Hampshire USA

Nationalities of student attendees:

Belgium	Indonesia
Dutch Netherlands Antilles (Saba)	Italy
France	Mexico
Germany	United States
India	

"Youth Accord On Biodiversity" January, 2005 El Eden Ecological Reserve, Quintana Roo, Mexico

Preamble

We are today's tomorrow. What happens today does not just affect the future, it *is* the future. There are plants and animals living today that have not yet been discovered, that may never be discovered, because of our carelessness and thoughtless aspirations. We need to allow for the existence of all species on this planet.

All species have a right to live. Only humans destroy the Earth and annihilate entire species in our quest for comfort and power. It is up to us as one species on this planet – and in particular to the people in power - to stop the harm that is being done to the world. When any local or global decision must be made, we need to consider each option's potential impact on the environment. Countries will go to war, leaders will be assassinated, people will starve and overthrow their governments, and terrorist attacks will be made. However, after all of this, nations, societies, and cultures will try to be pieced back together and people will continue to hope for a better future. The Earth cannot any longer fix itself. The best way to save our home is to save it now. Your decisions as international leaders are *our* future and the future of millions of plants and animals. Please make the right ones for our future's future.

Our work together as an international group of students respectfully requests you to include our voice in your important work. We submit the following considerations for hope … for all … for the future.

Youth Accord On Biodiversity

- The earth is a beautiful diverse planet on which humankind lives as a part of nature. Nature is a gift that needs to be cherished because it provides the three necessities: food, water, and shelter. It also must be around for future generations to enjoy. Therefore, it is necessary to conserve what is left of it. What happens to the environment should be closely monitored and regulated.

- Set a common international goal to conserve biodiversity. The decisions of the global community as a whole have the influence and the power to change things now. Anything that is to be changed environmentally needs to be a global effort. The people will notice if the government starts funding more to environmental efforts and they will follow. Without the influence of the government there will never be a large impact.

- Change is needed to preserve the beauty of nature meaning that new laws, funding for equipment, research, and informing the community about the cycle of life which includes all creatures and plants is necessary.

- Encourage people by issuing tax incentives to organizations that promote and use positive conservation skills.
- Make it easier to recycle by putting recycling bins around public places throughout the world and support recycling programs.
- Support Government funding for water purification.
- Support Government funding towards technology that has a low environmental impact.
- Promotion of conservation efforts, volunteers for conservation organizations, awareness towards the destruction of natural habitats, the training of teachers about environmental information, teaching children about nature, and remembering that they are the ones who will inherit the earth.
- Education is the key to understanding the importance of conserving biodiversity. Education for the youth about the environment is needed at a larger scale since they are the ones who will be responsible for it when we

are gone. It gives youth around the world an opportunity to come together to experience the environment and express their concerns about what is happening to it as well.

- Promote learning in the classroom (grade 1-6) about recycling, nature hiking, and other community activities that are healthy for the environment. Promote in classrooms (grades 7-12) for the older students to teach the younger students by running these programs.

- All living things have the right to exist. To exist they need food, clean water, clean air and natural habitats. Species become endangered and then extinct. It is necessary to protect them before they become endangered. If one species is hurt or destroyed, then the rest of the species around them will also suffer because they depend on each other like we depend on them to survive.

- Waste management and energy efficiency need more restrictions so that companies and consumers have guidelines to improve our pollution situation. Politics on emissions such as CO_2 and other greenhouse gasses need to be stricter to maintain the environment. Pollution damages the ozone layer and instigates global warming. The reverse or slowing of the process of global warming will help preserve the habitats, ecosystems, the species that live there, and prevent the destruction of the planet

- Acid rain is caused by toxic chemicals that are evaporated with the water that become rain, this rain destroys trees and the other living things that it comes in contact with; therefore, it is necessary to find a new way to filter the emissions of smokestacks, power plants, and cars which should reduce the amount of acid rain.

- Set development restrictions as a small step to help protect and preserve many of the natural habitats left in or near urban areas. Make sure that the human population does not surpass the carrying capacity of the land on which homes are being built. Encourage the use of environmentally safe construction materials.

- Regulate deforestation so that it is not as damaging to the environment because it not only destroys the trees, but the birds, insects, and other organisms that live on them and around them.

- Protect the coral reefs and the ocean's ecosystem more strictly from over-fishing, pollution, and the other problems that occur through the meddling of humankind in the ocean. People as well as millions of animals and other organisms depend on the life in the reefs and ocean for their survival. The reefs also protect the islands and coastlines from hurricanes and other violent storms and the ocean supplies much of the world's oxygen.

- Keep a close eye on ecotourism which is alright until it begins to damage the delicate environment that hosts it.

- Support restraint from disturbing the natural events on the planet.

- Maintain balance on earth by saving the ecosystems that organisms live in. Open spaces need to be saved from development and other forms of destruction because the organisms that live there support us.

- We need to conduct more research on what is happening to our environment. New medicines, alternatives for environmentally endangering products, and other discoveries come from the studies of plants and organisms that have been discovered. Also, we need to conserve all organisms so that we may continue to search for new species because so many have not yet been discovered.

Summary: The crisis of global biodiversity does not lie in nature, it lies within mankind. Mankind must become aware of what we are doing to our planet. Laws and regulations are a step in the right direction but are not enough to change our world's fate. To change the global perception, we must become aware of not only our actions, but the consequences resulting thereof. Conserving biodiversity is our future! We are in this together. We must unite our efforts to rescue our world, for it is the only home we have. As a part of nature, humans must willingly and consciously unify to conserve and honor the gift of nature.

Section 4:
Intellectual
Engagement

Dandelions, elephants, and the ecology of interdisciplinary curriculum

E cologists look for patterns and then try to interpret them. Organisms self-replicate and the very fact that they do is one characteristic that separates living from nonliving or never-living. One such observable pattern is the relative number of offspring a species leaves behind as its legacy.

To an ecologist, the pattern is represented as "r-selection" or "k-selection." That is to say, an organism (such as a dandelion) may put a lot of energy into producing large numbers of offspring (r-selection) and little if any energy into caring for their young. This strategy bets on a few will survive no matter what. K-selection (we will scale to and use an elephant as the example here) is a strategy where only a few offspring are produced but more energy is put into care and or rearing the offspring to ensure success. Both strategies make sense and enable the next generation of that species to continue in our biosphere. It is a pattern packed with ecology and evolution.

Similarly, whether or not curriculum should be interdisciplinary needs to be examined under the lens of what makes sense too. Curriculum is also packed with ecology and evolution.

An example of an evolutionary curriculum flop then flip...

I was most fortunate to be hired in a rural public school in New Hampshire that had a principal who dared to push educational boundaries. What the school district lacked in funding was more than compensated by faculty who were intentional about what they brought to their professional practice.

Dennis, our principal, gave three of us the challenge and opportunity to develop a school within a school for about 60 high school students. We would have the students for 4 hours each day. It was up to us on how we structured those four hours.

Val (English), Julie (mathematics), and myself (science) were excited and naïve about how to bring this to fruition. Although we agreed on a name for our program quickly .... Spectrum, our initial curriculum work was arduous and flawed.

The name "Spectrum" gave us a vision for our work to be inclusive and it was summer. We had the luxury of time to work collaboratively, read a few "good books" together to think about the big ideas we would teach together, and reflect. Daily, we came together to discuss our ideas and write curriculum that merged our three disciplines.

We discovered that good versus soggy interdisciplinary curriculum is an earned phenomenon. We were three weeks into writing some very soggy curriculum when we came to the realization that what we had was a very contrived piece of work. We were focused on making every lesson interdisciplinary … each hour … each day.

Each of us were regarded as "good teachers" with deep content knowledge. Ironically, we believed at first that our passion for our content area was a weakness rather than a strength that we needed to overcome to engage students. However, what we had produced up until this point was a grand flop!

Our interdisciplinary work thus far lacked passion, substance, and engagement. Those were the very three qualities that we were hoping to get at! That realization was disappointing but important for us (and our future students).

Turning a flop to the beginnings of a flipped hit …

Dissecting our soggy curriculum, we discovered through conversations and reflection that to get at our passion for our discipline we need to start there. What was it that brought Val to love English, Julie math, and Dan, science? That was a much-needed conversation and led to us developing a Venn diagram depicting our beloved disciplines.

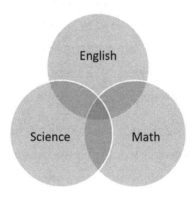

Each of us listed the core values, beliefs, ideas of our discipline and then had intelligent discussion of where true interdisciplinary connections would occur. Sometimes it might mean an English-science connection (no math), other times an English-math connection (no science) or any of the 2 disciplines and even sometimes even all three. And yes, there would be times left just for the solo discipline as well.

This is not to say that good interdisciplinary work cannot occur until students have been fed a domain rich diet, but rather a realization that students need the threads of experience in specific domains before they may weave a quality fabric. Both domain-rich and interdisciplinary connections compliment one another and enable students to construct meaning and new knowledge.

We started out trying to purge ourselves from the r-selection ("more is more") content driven curriculum and get to a k-selection ("less is more") nurtured and rich opportunity for our students. In the end, we realized both are needed in moderation and more importantly, in a context that makes sense. The ecology and evolution of curriculum is packed and needs to be unpacked with a respectful understanding of the tinkering.

So how does this respectful tinkering come about?

It begins with teacher "authorship" of their curriculum. There is an abundance of well-intentioned prepackaged curriculum out there. All connected to various state and national standards. I worry about this.

When schools and school districts buy or contract with curriculum providers and expect teachers not to go off script, they have replaced the profession of teachers who are creative artists and intellectuals with the notion of "teachers as technicians." What is at stake is the loss of creative, intelligent, and imaginative professionals who often create intuitive curriculum that has the local and even global community flavor that hooks student inquiry and engagement.

When I was a secondary science coordinator and teacher, I would look for certain qualities in a teacher candidate when we were hiring faculty (I shared these qualities with my per-service graduate students who would soon be looking for teaching positions. It was a two-way street—apply to schools that value these qualities I would tell them.). First, I searched for individuals who knew their discipline content well enough to be playful with the content and secondly, someone who enjoys working with youth.

Putting smart and playful teachers together to develop and write curriculum is what Aldo Leopold called "intelligent tinkering" in a conservation biology land ethic. This is what we need more now than ever. Whether teachers are working together on interdisciplinary curricular themes or by themselves within their discipline domains, they need to create curriculum that encompasses richness, complexity, and ambiguity. Context and content both matter. Biologists often cite "form follows function." If our function as educators is to assist students in becoming lifelong learners, capable of dealing with complex decisions and understandings of how our "world" works, then we need to reexamine the form in which we deliver both content and context.

"It is what it is and it isn't what it isn't."

After presenting a workshop on developing inquiry-based curriculum at a teacher conference, I overheard several of the participants talking about my workshop. "He can do that because he teaches in a poor and rural community. The parents don't care." A decade later, after presenting a similar workshop at another conference, I overheard "He can do that because he teaches in a rich suburban community. He has the resources and parent support."

These two seemingly distinct and opposite "takeaways" by participants in similar workshops remind me of what a well-known NFL football coach stated during a press conference: "It is what it is and it isn't what it isn't." I use that quote to dissect meaning from what appear to be very disparate conversations about the same workshop.

Whether I was teaching in the rural community, early in my career, or in that suburban community years later, I found that "it is what it is" in the following ways:

1. In both contexts, and regardless of their backgrounds, the students were engaged as "young scientists."

2. My students and their parents trusted me. Students were encouraged to talk about their classroom experiences in class with their parents, and, in fact they did on a regular basis.

3. And perhaps most importantly, classes were both rigorous and joyful.

So then, "what isn't it?"

In both settings, it was not about available resources or related to the particular demographics of a zip code.

Digging deeper.

Creating curriculum and lesson plans is a creative process. In many respects, it is an art form as well as an intellectual process—one that, as teachers, we need to continually be engaged with. On my work desk at home sits "my little black book," which in truth is neither black nor little. It is a tattered multicolored cloth-covered flip open style notebook with sticky notes, scraps of paper covered in notes, and pages of handwritten questions gleaned from "moments." Those moments arise from reading an article, a book, a poem, or hearing an interview (TV, radio), talking with friends, attending a lecture, etc. The resulting ideas might lead to a key question to frame a curriculum project; or suggest an intriguing start to a lesson plan; or simply remain in my notebook for later inspiration. In other words, some of these become the DNA for my future projects or lesson plans while others are still "aging."

As a teacher developing a lesson plan, I want to create situations where students can surprise themselves and me. That translates to teaching science as science is done. This framework is messy and unscripted. However, if it is scaffolded by a teacher who has both the background content and pedagogical skills, the outcome will be success.

The teacher becomes a mentor rather than an expert passively imparting knowledge to an audience of students. The teacher/mentor guides and often may redirect students in this learning environment. They may point or open a door to new avenues to explore by asking probing questions as their young scientists move forward in their explorations.

"What do you think?" "Why do you think that?" "Can you tell me more?" How do you know this?" "What questions do you still have?"

Later in my career as a teacher and mentor of future science educators, I would give them a small card with a list of questions that I called "conversation starters" on it. I would tell them to keep that card handy when they were leading a lab or field lesson with their students. Sometimes, especially as novice educators with so much to keep your eyes and ears on during a class, you can lose track of important conversations to have with your students as they are working. This can be a perfect time for them to move from student to student and ask those questions rather than just managing the lab or field experience. Consult that card and begin a conversation.

Other than the questions that I listed above, other conversation starters may include:

All inquiry projects start with students first brainstorming and listing "What does a scientist do?" That class list remains posted as their student research projects move forward. We will circle back to that list once their projects are completed, and I ask my students to reflect on how they were scientists during their project work. This self-assessment is critical. Students make meaning of their project work through the scientific processes they undertook during their own scientific endeavor. This is where both the rigor and joy become evident.

* * *

This process is not limited to inquiry-based projects.

A pedagogical focus teaching science today is centered on using phenomena at the center of inquiry engagement. Phenology and seasonal change, the migration of species, global climate change, bioethics are a few examples that are rich areas for students to explore and make discoveries. A second and important strand that has emerged in science education's current pedagogical evolution is fostering student engineering practices. Instead of phenomena, students use engineering practices to solve problems.

Once again, substituting "engineering practices" for what do "scientists do" in an initial brainstorm session with students works. The Next Generation Science Standards uses the following attributes in answering what do scientists and engineers do.

- Defining problems.
- Developing and using models.
- Planning and carrying out investigations.
- Analyzing and interpreting data.
- Using mathematics and computational thinking.
- Designing solutions.

- Engaging in argument from evidence.
- Obtaining, evaluating, and communicating information

The teacher as mentor continues to use conversation starters (those pesky questions to probe student learning) with their students as they work on their problem-solving project work.

By the way, that NFL football coach that I quoted was Bill Belichick.

Lesson Plans Do Not Improve After 10 P.M.

As they are about to take off in search of an endangered African species, the late adventurer and author, Doug Adams, in his book *Last Chance To See*, hears and transcribes his bush pilot's message from the cockpit:

"We commend our lives into Thy hands, O Lord."

While it may not be the sort of statement you want to hear from your pilot as his hand is reaching for the throttle, it does frame a reflective ritual for the pilot as he begins a very well-planned task. That ritual conveys a humble acknowledgement that, despite a flight plan, "things may change."

Similarly, you may be completely prepared as you enter the classroom, however you have no idea what one, two, or more students may be bringing to that classroom on that day at that time. The best you can do is have a good night's sleep and perhaps a reflective ritual (not necessarily a prayer), as your teaching day begins. Whatever the ritual, it should be a humble reminder that your lesson plan has a dimension that you have no control over ... your students' state of mind that day ... among other variables. The lesson may flow perfectly. Bravo! Be humble, that may not be the case the next time you use it (next period or next year). In-flight corrections are almost always needed as your lesson unfolds. And yes, in some cases, that lesson may just simply need to be scratched.

There is no such thing as a perfect lesson plan. None the less, lesson plans may improve with age via reflection and revision (more on this in a later essay).

One of my favorite responsibilities in my role as director of science education is "mentoring" my graduate students through their first teaching practicum. Certainly, a significant part of my role is teaching them methods in science teaching. However, the artful and diplomatic role includes reading and commenting on their lesson plans as well as observing and offering critique of their lessons with students. Regarding the latter, I quickly learned to set an important parameter for my students ... lesson plans were to be submitted to me for review and comment by 8:00 PM. This would allow time for revision before 10 PM, signaling a time for all to get some rest. Lesson plans do not improve after 10 PM.

My pre-service teachers, graduate students, all strove for perfection. Ironically, this desire for perfection inevitably would lead to disappointment upon delivery of the lesson and consequently morph into self-doubt about whether or not they can teach. These are very smart, caring, and passionate students who are desperately needed to fill classrooms. Each one of my students is unique but they share a common denominator and at least one disposition. All were excellent students leading up to their graduate studies and they subconsciously held an unintended frame of self-reference that all students learn the same way they did. A few weeks into teaching their first practicum, both of those precepts are challenged.

My students are not alone.

Nationally, we have an unprecedented exit … departure from the teaching profession by year 1-5 teachers. In fact, current research is showing an increasing rate in mid-career teachers leaving the profession as well. Why? What is causing this exodus from a noble profession where most entered hoping to make a difference in children's lives?

The unrelenting state and national reforms since *A Nation at Risk* (1983) was published has arguably added to the hastened departure of many seasoned teaching professionals and causing pause for those who may be considering teaching as a profession.

Although well intentioned, these "one size fixes all problems" reform platforms offer a simplistic "silver bullet" mechanistic roadmap whereas education is a multifaceted, multidimensional, and human endeavor. Perfect curriculum, perfect lessons cannot be mandated. Many of the thinkers, authors, and developers of these platforms did not have the advantage my graduate pre-service teachers have … to teach others in a teaching practicum. Thereby, their notions of how students learn where never challenged. They too, hold the unintended frame of self-reference that all students learn in the same way they did.

Not surprisingly, seasoned and new to the profession teachers are overwhelmed with these new initiatives as they attend yet another professional development training on implementation of the next reform platform. Soon follows disappointment and frustration when the latest student achievement test scores fail to meet a bar set on naïve and overly simplistic and mechanistic attributes. Blame and finger pointing follows …

There is no one perfect fix or perfect lesson plan. There is no perfect curriculum or set of standards. We are setting up both experienced and novice teachers with a mucky mire that reinforces self-doubt in good teachers as well as the profession.

We need more joy in teaching, which translates to more joy in the classroom. Without joy we will not have a transformative pathway to innovation, inspiration, or lifelong learning for students and teachers. What is needed is not a "fix" but an attitude adjustment and good, solid mentoring of new teachers. Trusting the professionals, that is teachers, to share their joy and passion for their discipline with children will go a very long way in transforming all children's lives.

Before joining the teacher education faculty at a university, I was a high school teacher. When we were hiring a new faculty member, I used three lenses when interviewing candidates. Did the candidate know her/ his subject well enough to be playful (and thereby joyful) with the content? Did the candidate genuinely enjoy working with children? Is this candidate reflective, knowing that making mistakes and changing that lesson/ flight plan is part of good teaching? With good mentoring (the other important facet to longevity in the profession), new faculty can be taught methodology.

Attitude is a more challenging characteristic to coach or mentor.

Back to my pre-service graduate students and their quest for lesson perfection. During our end of week Friday afternoon debriefing sessions, I literally introduced a "rubber chicken" to our conversation of how things went during their week of teaching. For twenty minutes or so, students had the opportunity to highlight one thing that did not go well during their week teaching. It became an opportunity to reflect, smile at one's mistakes, and grow. Everyone had at least one rubber chicken moment during the week to share … including me. We learned to smile at ourselves and discovered that better days of teaching had followed. One student would take home that rubber chicken trophy reminder for the week to give it to another colleague the following Friday. This simple ritual kept everyone humble, honest, and sane.

(At their graduation, I would give every one of my students a rubber chicken to take with them. Not surprisingly, I continue to receive email "rubber chicken moments" from many as they continue to share their passion and humanness with their students.)

Non-planned, non-scheduled teachable and even non-teachable moments are brought into our classroom each day and present themselves in a variety of ways. A student issue, a current event, an equipment or prop malfunction, fire drill, are among the many ways a lesson plan will go awry. These will always present a challenge to that perfect lesson and always an opportunity to examine what makes us human. Although they may confound the perfect lesson, it is possible they may also lead to enduring understandings that were not a part of our original lesson plan but lead to a valuable lesson.

Yes, in all probability, Doug Adams was more than likely concerned hearing his pilot's routine. However, his pilot was very well prepared ... humbly acknowledging that possibilities to challenge his flight plan and training are always present. He understood that some in-flight changes may be needed for all to have that successful flight. As educators, we too need to have a pre-class lesson reflective mantra ... a lesson plan is not perfect, some in-flight redirection may be needed. Lesson plans do not improve after 10 PM and the profession of teaching needs to have the support and understanding that the "in-flight" changes are more important than the scripted curriculum that supplants professional training, insight, joy of learning, and ultimately student achievement.

How do you assess "academic swagger"?

Transitions. Although I was by now teaching at a university, I continued to lead occasional biodiversity field projects in the Yucatán for high school students and teachers. Continuing work with high school students segued my transition from one educational setting into the other. Certainly, this new professional opportunity afforded me new and welcomed challenges. It also added to my perspective of the learning continuum .... mine included.

Four years into my career as a university professor, I was sipping coffee waiting in a Mexican coastal community for another group of high school students to arrive and begin our biodiversity research project together. The group arrived and during introductions, one student asked if it is true that the Maya calendar states that the world will end December 2012 (popular press outlets and social media had been playing this up that year). Quickly, and with a wry smile, another student responded that his Pringles chips don't expire until 2013 so it couldn't be true. Everyone laughed enjoying that parody and prophecy of expiration dates.

That comment brought me back to why it took me almost two full weeks to decide whether or not I would accept the position offered by Brown's Department of Education.

When you hear comments such as the one mentioned, you realize that you are engaged with young minds poised between childhood and adulthood. Transition.

As an educator, it is exciting to be at least one moderator in that often-turbulent adolescent transition. As a science educator, I found it a necessity to create learning situations where students have an opportunity to uncover misconceptions and challenge their preconceptions of how our world works. We need to meet students where they are but not let them stay there.

One example of this "uncovering" of misconceptions follows.

A night hike is always exciting and usually raises the adrenaline levels in my students as we look for nocturnal insects, reptiles, and mammals in the forest. The darkness is especially deep under a thick canopy of leaves. Colleagues who never ventured into the field with students always marveled at my willingness and intentionality of getting high school students outside and often in tropical forests. They were concerned about the potential shenanigans adolescents may bring along to the experience. I contend that darkness is the greatest chaperone to have on your side while traveling with students in a tropical forest. Once the sun sets, students would close in on adults like heat-seeking missiles.

One evening, while off a trail looking at a moth that had lighted on a tree, I overheard one student say, "Uh-oh, we are off the trail. How do we find our way back to it?" I responded that we have our compasses, and we will use them to make our way back. The student then countered, "But the sun set. A compass won't work."

Somehow and somewhere during her learning journey, this student had thought the Earth's magnetic field set along with sun each evening. It is worth noting that this was a very bright and motivated student. In fact, today she has a PhD in environmental science.

How do we uncover misconceptions if we do not test ideas and concepts through real application? My personal journals are filled with similar examples of student misconceptions that were only brought to light via field or real-world applications.

Real-world applications also enable students to use the academic jargon and skills in a meaningful context. A note in my journal reminds me of the following story…

Parker did not strike me as a particular religious or spiritual young person. One day, as we were leaving a forest where we had just set up a biodiversity plot, he was beaming. Smiling, joking, and chatting with his classmates, I overheard him say, "I bet in heaven, all the trees have a DBH of 10 cm and every stick you pick up is 1.3 meters long."

What he was referring to were the protocols for our field work that day. We were only measuring the diameter at breast height (DBH) of trees that were 10 cm or greater at 1.3 meters above the ground. Trees with less than a 10 cm DBH were not included in our survey. To make our work more efficient, we would search for a stick on the ground that was 1.3 meters long to place aside the trees we would measure.

Parker found his field biology swagger that morning. He was using newly acquired academic vocabulary and skills in a most appropriate and humorous way. He not only "got it" but now owned this knowledge and skill set enough to transfer it to an amusing application.

Parker's statement, in many ways, was a true assessment of his work that morning. How do you measure or quantify that?

Our present national educational obsession is to evaluate students, teachers, and even schools through "assessments." Developing assessment instruments is thorny and rife with keep it simple and cost effective. This unfortunately translates into one-dimensional tests that do a good job of quantifying objective data but fails to capture the swagger in Parker's statement or the aha of a student turning a misconception into a conception of how our world works.

A quick review of how we got here.

Academic assessment has also seen several transitions in the past several decades.

In 1983, The Nation at Risk report claimed that our education system had failed us. To paraphrase the report: "The educational foundations of our society are presently being eroded by a rising tide of mediocrity that threatens our very future as a Nation and a people... If an unfriendly foreign power had attempted to impose on America the mediocre educational performance that exists today, we might well have viewed it as an act of war."

A new post-Sputnik education reform reboot was taking form. These emerging versions would now link student assessments with teacher evaluation and school validation.

The Nation at Risk report gave birth to several blue-ribbon education commissions, including a Governor's Task Force and the American Association for the Advancement of Science (Science for all Americans) tasked to fix this. Others, including professional education associations (NSTA, NCTM, NCTM), became early adopters in this emerging dialogue often targeting public education and the need to create "standards." State by state, education standards were developed, which led to the inevitable question of "how do we measure how well students meet these standards?" Comparing international test score results in science and mathematics (TIMMS) became a national pastime for politicians. Students in the United States did not fare well when compared to other developed nations.

Yet, there were and are closer to home questions that need and still need to be addressed.

Is it surprising to see that students in more affluent suburban communities outperform their peers in rural or inner-city schools? Is it surprising to see teacher turnover in rural and urban schools so much greater than in the suburbs? How surprising is it to see our best and brightest college and graduate students choose fields other than education given how teachers are valued in our society? Currently, 40% of year 1 to 5 teachers leave the profession within that time span. While these systemic issues have been understood for a long period of time, few potential solutions have been implemented in public education. Instead, we have tried a variety of tweaks that do not address the interconnected nature of these systemic issues. Equitable funding for schools, valuing educators as we do commensurate professions, thereby increasing the prestige and, dare I say, salaries of teachers.

Instead of taking on those more difficult questions, we answered with "No Child Left Behind" legislation. This legislation sacrificed the natural inquisitiveness of children and further gutted the profession of teaching as a profession, on the altar of testing. Tying standardized testing to funding schools as well as a measure of teacher accountability moved public education in the wrong direction.

We need more intelligent, creative, and passionate people to become teachers. We need good storytellers, artists, inquisitive minds who passionately care about children and their future to enter the profession. Individuals whose curriculum innovations illustrate concepts, meaningful connections, and common experiences with learning. We need individuals who put together this type of integrative pedagogy that fosters assessments FOR learning versus assessment OF learning.

Assessments that allow for students to surprise us and themselves with their newly acquired academic swagger or aha moments.

End Note:

This was an email I sent to my last MAT cohort during my final semester of teaching.

Dear MATs / Class of 2017,

Today, at noon, an event occurred that compels me to write to all of you. Some of you may disagree with me and what I am about to write, and I welcome that and expect that. After all, critical thought is what democracy and education is all about.

I cannot keep silent regarding my shock over the appointment of our new Education Czar, Betsy Devos. We cannot let public education in our nation take a back seat on the bus for what has been the hallmark of our nation's progress through growing pains of over the past two centuries and now regress. We have come far … with those growing pains that sometimes saw setbacks but always moving forward with thoughtful and free expression to correct and redirect us. It has not been perfect, but the conversations, free protests, and will of individuals to speak for all has persisted and guided us a nation to do the right thing.

As one person, I can speak for the difference public education has made in my life. I was the first person in my family (both on my mom's and dad's sides) to graduate from high school and then college. My parents valued education and made sure that my two younger brothers and I went to school every day. I am so appreciative of that AND the public-school teachers that I had grades 1-12 that saw me as a "science nerd" and truly helped me navigate an unlikely path to become a teacher. College did not seem accessible, given the cost. My public-school teachers and a guidance counselor made the difference enabling me to receive a full scholarship.

Here I am, 40 years later, about to retire from what I know is the best profession anyone can aspire to and I have to thank the public schools for that. Take a breath and look at your students. You will be making that difference for so many of your future students!

Most of you know me and know that I like to tell stories … so one last story in this too long email:

Last December I had the opportunity to run some "PD" for a Boston public school. I arrived early on a very cold day (3 degrees F) and watched kids running into school as I arrived. As I was setting up in a classroom, I watched a young teacher—despite the "normal morning chaos" of taking attendance, with countless interruptions and announcements on the speaker ... notice her students. Any student coming into her class who did not have a hat or gloves, she called to her desk and offered them a new hat / gloves from a pile she brought in that cold morning. She knew her students and was prepared to care for them. There is no teacher evaluation that I know of that scores that and yet, that is what is needed most. She notices and cares for her kids and has the content and pedagogical knowledge to empower those kids to dream big.

You need to know, that after 40 years in our wonderful profession, that I would do it all over again.

Wishing all of you the best this semester!
Love,
Dan

Glossary

(acronyms used in the essays):

CES (Coalition of Essential Schools) - The Coalition of Essential Schools is a US organization created to further a type of whole-school reform originally envisioned by founder Ted Sizer in his book *Horace's Compromise*. http://essentialschools.org/

NABT (National Association of Biology Teachers) - The National Association of Biology Teachers is an incorporated association of biology educators in the United States. It was initially founded in response to the poor understanding of biology and the decline in the teaching of the subject in the 1930s.   https://nabt.org/

NCTM (National Council of Teacher of Mathematics) - Founded in 1920, The National Council of Teachers of Mathematics is the world's largest mathematics education organization. NCTM holds annual national and regional conferences for teachers and publishes five journals. https://www.nctm.org/

NSTA (National Science Teaching Association) - The National Science Teaching Association, founded in 1944 and headquartered in Arlington, Virginia, is an association of science teachers in the United States and is the largest organization of science teachers worldwide. https://www.nsta.org/

PD (Professional Development) - Professional development is learning to earn or maintain professional credentials such as academic degrees to formal coursework, attending conferences, and informal learning opportunities situated in practice.

PLC (Professional Learning Community) - A professional learning community is a method to foster collaborative learning among colleagues within a particular work environment or field. It is often used in schools as a way to organize teachers into working groups of practice-based professional learning.

STEM / STEAM (Science Technology Engineering Math / Science Technology Engineering Art Math) - STEM is a broad term used to group together these academic disciplines. This term is typically used to address an education policy or curriculum choices in schools. STEAM is an educational approach that incorporates the arts into the more familiar STEM model, which includes science, technology, engineering, and mathematics. STEAM programs can include any of the visual or performing arts, such as dance, design, painting, photography, and writing.

TIMMS (Trends in International Mathematics and Science Study) - Trends in International Mathematics and Science Study is a series of international assessments of the mathematics and science knowledge of students around the world. TIMSS data have been collected from students at grades 4 and 8 every 4 years since 1995, with the United States participating in every administration of TIMSS.

A Methods & Pedagogy For Teaching Matrix:

Discipline → Pedagogy ↓ Methodology→	X-Disciplinary	Science / Mathematics	Science Literacy & Numeracy
Classroom Discussion	• Graffiti Boards • Carousel • Paper Pass • Read and Feed • 2 Cent Discussion • Save the Last Word for Me • Conversational Round Table • Socratic Seminar • Read-around • Whip	• Socratic Seminar (Data & Text) • Reciprocal Teaching • Carousel • Whip • Reading Response Chain • Consenso-gram • Fishbowl discussions • Experience Map • Debate	• Awareness of patterns of classroom talk such as IRE • Whole class discussion • Turn and talk • Discussion protocols • Small group/cross group/whole group discussion structure
Cooperative Learning	• Reciprocal Teaching (parts of this in other areas of chart) • Tea Party • Literature circles/reading groups • Arts Literacy Strategies: sculpture garden, handshakes, tableaux • Anticipation guidesPeer review	• Jigsaw • Arts Literacy Strategies: sculpture garden, handshakes, tableaux • KWL • Simulations • Found Poetry • Think-Pair-Share	• Discussion summary • Preparing and managing guidelines for sharing student work • Small group/cross group/whole group discussion structure

| Development of Student Skills | • Symbol Name Tags
• Dialogue Journals
• Target Notes
• Thinking-in-Threes
• Paragraph writing: I am organized, who are you?
• Questioning: Question Around, ReQuest, categorizing questions: right there, pulling it together, text and me, on my own.
• Life graph
• Other journals: response journals, logs, EQ journals, process journals, meta-cognitive journals

• Formula Poetry—Where I'm From, Providence, RI, Age Poems, Mirror Poems,
• Embellishing
• Interior Monologues
• Concept mapping
• Resource maps—8 square and long ago
• Summary writing

• Concept maps and graphic organizers, both teacher made, and student made
• Word sorts
• Mnemonics and other memory aids
Working with visual art | • Guided note taking
• Concept Maps
• Journals / Lab. Reports
• Inquiry Models – graduated inquiry projects.
• Drawing / Sketching
• Research Cycle & Conducting Surveys
• Think Aloud

• Concept maps and graphic organizers, both teacher made and student made
• Word sorts
• Mnemonics and other memory aids
• Working with visual art

• Questioning Designing instruction around Essential Questions; Devising questions based on the new Bloom's Taxonomy | • Arts Literacy Performance Cycle
• Observing/Assessing student literacy skills
• Fostering student meta-cognition
• Reading: pair/share Rehearse and read Choral reading Readers' theater Jump-in reading Final word Mark up and annotate texts: insert method and post-it notes Point-of view (schema) exercises

Analyzing text structures

• Writing: Writing process Do Now Entrance ticket Exit ticket Big exit ticket Journaling guidelines Note-taking guidelines Cornell notetaking "Talking back" to text Peer editing

• Concept maps and graphic organizers, both teacher made, and student made
• Word sorts
• Mnemonics and other memory aids
• Working with visual art |

| Direct Teacher Presentations | • Question-driven presentation
• Interactive presentation
• Multimedia presentation | • Using multimedia (ppt, SmartBoards, Elmo projectors)
• Question-driven presentation
• Interactive presentation (w/ DVD/ video) | • Managing student focus
• Directing students' attention
• Teaching with picture books |

Acknowledgement

A journey taken has a past, present, and future, especially in teaching. Every teacher needs that supportive community of family, friends, and colleagues through each phase of their professional career. Scribbling a note or a reflection in one's journal tends to be a solitary venture. However, reviewing and bringing them to a broader audience is not a solo event and I have been fortunate to have an encouraging cohort to bring past reflections and thoughts to current and future colleagues in this wonderful and most important profession. My debt of gratitude includes many more than just the few that follow.

Ralph Van Inwagen, Kurt Wootten – the whips, for encouraging and getting my writing started as initial editors and writing coaches.

"Dr. Bob" Mackin, Anne Clifton-Waite, and Robert Allwarden for their editorial insights and inspiration as educational teacher-leaders as well as the many other colleagues and friends at Souhegan High School.

Bil Johnson – offered insight on the economy of words and ultimately suggested one of my essay titles in naming the entire collection of reflections.

Steve Martin, Kat Jara, Kelly Budd, and Rebecca Veilleux. Teaching friends who make a difference each day with their students and provided valuable feedback for me to keep on track of what really matters as I worked on this.

The Department of Education at Brown University, especially my colleagues in teacher education, for giving me an opportunity to work with you. I learned so much from all of you.

El Eden Ecological Reserve (Quintana Roo, Mexico); Marco Lazcano, Juan Castillo, and Cristina MacSweeny-Gonzales for their support of my HabitatNet project and our many discussions and laughs with one another over the years.

My students, going back to 1976 up through to 2017 who taught me how to teach. Thank you.

Upward Bound – St. Lawrence University and the Akwesasne Nation as well as the Perkiomen School (Pennsburg, PA), for giving me an opportunity to start my career as a novice teacher with a lot to learn.

Most importantly, with over-the-top gratitude to my family, thank you. Dear Mame, Meghan, Kerry, and Nora; you have unselfishly supported my affair with education over the decades that included sharing a variety of specimens in our freezer for my classes, countless family trips to collect bugs, plants, animal sign (aka scat), and field time with my students. Thank you. I love you.

Finally, Jamie Anderson at Gatekeeper Press, who assisted me through this process of getting these very rough journal notes and reflections published. Thank you.